THE LITTLE TREASURY

The Lockert Library of Poetry in Translation

Editorial Adviser: John Frederick Nims

For other titles in the Lockert Library see page 105.

THE LITTLE TREASURY OF ONE HUNDRED PEOPLE, ONE POEM EACH

Compiled by
Fujiwara no Sadaie (1162-1241)

Translated by Tom Galt

Princeton University Press
Princeton, New Jersey

Copyright © 1982 by Princeton University Press
Published by Princeton University Press, 41 William Street, Princeton, New Jersey
In the United Kingdom: Princeton University Press, Guildford, Surrey

All Rights Reserved
Library of Congress Cataloging in Publication Data will be found on the
last printed page of this book

The Lockert Library of Poetry in Translation is supported by a bequest
from Charles Lacy Lockert (1888-1974)

This book has been composed in Linotron Bembo
The calligraphy is by Hiroko Yoshikawa

Clothbound editions of Princeton University Press books are printed on acid-free
paper, and binding materials are chosen for strength and durability

Printed in the United States of America by Princeton University
Press, Princeton, New Jersey

To Yoko Kawashima Watkins

川島擁子さんへ

without whose patience and resourcefulness this book would not have been possible.

CONTENTS

Acknowledgments   ix
Introduction   xi
The Little Treasury   xiii
An Index and Glossary of Poets   101

ACKNOWLEDGMENTS

The poems and translations on pages 1, 2, 3, 5, 9, and 11 originally appeared in *Buckle* (Fall/Winter 1981); those on pages 27, 28, 31, 32, 33, and 35 first appeared, with somewhat shorter commentaries, in *Phoebe* (Winter 1980).

INTRODUCTION

Most Japanese of my acquaintance know all these poems by heart. I encountered them first as a card game. For this a hundred cards, each bearing only the last two lines of a five-line poem, are spread out on a tatami mat of a Japanese-style floor. Facing the players sits the reader—usually a mother who is hostess at this party—with another set of cards in piles, face down, each containing a whole poem. Cutting the piles, she takes up one at random to read aloud.

At once each player tries to guess which poem it is and to grab the card containing the last two lines. If necessary, mother will read the whole poem twice, but the second reading may be only to settle disputes. At least one lady has told me that when young she was forbidden to play this game wearing a new kimono, as the players became so excited they tore their sleeves.

I had the good luck to buy unusually pretty cards, for the reader's set is decorated with portraits of all the poets. These are drawn largely from imagination, though through the centuries traditions have grown up as to how each should look. Similarly there are diverse tales about the poets, including those of whom nothing is known.

On the exact text and meaning of most of these poems the authoritative books heaped about my desk are in disaccord. Modern scholarship, moreover, demands newly understood verb endings and an updated way of writing them. The abundant puns and words with extra overtones often make possible four or five quite dissimilar translations of one tanka.

The selection was made (probably) by Fujiwara no Sadaie (1162-1241), a high Court official who, like his father before him, served as tutor to the imperial family, especially teaching them the art of poetry. Much later the collection was made into a card game because of its merit. In particular he had a good ear for poetic harmonies and was often in disputes with other Court officials because of his preference for variety in the methods, moods, and subject matters expressed.

Since this *Ogura Hyaku Nin Isshu* has been discussed in English reference books under various titles in English, the one used here is a word-for-word rendering. In the original, *Ogura* refers to *Ogura Yama* "Little Treasury Hill," so named for its shape, where the anthologist is said to have painted these tanka on the panels of shoji screens for his family, and expresses also the contrast between this little collection, a holiday pastime, and his two great compilations made in 1206 and in 1234 for the imperial library. In this one he could garner just his favorites.

The form of these poems may be called tanka or waka, and the translations given here are in this form, which is determined by syllable count. At various times various usages or theories, often quite dogmatic, have distinguished the words: that waka was once a series of lines with syllabic count 5-7-5 alternating with lines counting 7-7, this series running to any length, each of the five-line sections being a tanka; or that waka and tanka became alike in form though in one the break in grammar was after the third line, in the other after the second line; or that in one the sounds of the first triad are picked up in the final couplet, in the other they are not. Various schools also tell us what a poet is allowed to write about, and what tone must be maintained in tanka and what tone in waka.

However, Japanese dictionaries now give the two words as synonyms. And in this *Ogura*, the most famous collection of them ever made, the poets break their grammar where they please, build sonal patterns as their artistic sense demands, write about everything in their experience and in their thoughts, and scream, whisper, weep, laugh, like human beings.

THE LITTLE TREASURY

1

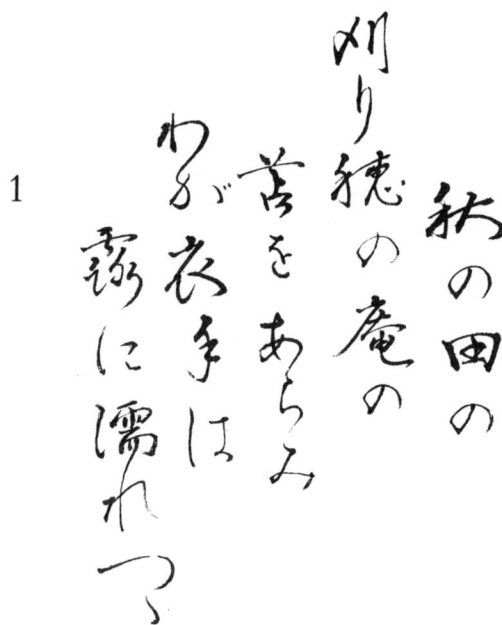

Aki no ta no
Kariho no iho no
　Toma wo arami
Waga koromode wa
Tsuyu ni nure tsutsu

　　Emperor Tenchi (626-671)

　　　　Lying on the rough
　　　Mats of the rice-harvest guards
　　　　In the autumn fields,
　　　I find the sleeves of my robe
　　　Wet. Is the dew so heavy?

Since damp sleeves always represent tears, the poem as usual means more than it says. Traveling, His Majesty was caught by nightfall and lodged in a temporary hut set up by farmers at harvest time. His councilors had not told him that his peasants, after scratching a meager crop from the soil, were not only heavily taxed by the nobles but must also keep watch, guarding their poor harvest against thieves, whom his government had done little to suppress. The discovery was a shock to him.

2

Haru sugite
Natsu ki ni kerashi
　Shirotae no
Koromo hosu chō
Ama no kagu yama
　　　Empress Jitō (645-702)

　　　　　　　　Spring already gone,
　　　　　　And summer is upon us
　　　　　　　　Too soon, as always,
　　　　For there the white garments air
　　　Against Perfume Bottle Hill.

As she is known for her sense of humor, we may suppose her quite sophisticatedly using the word *shirotae*, "white mysteries," for underrobes. The little mountain derived its name from its shape. Often in this book the place-name inspires the poem, and here the many layers of clothes, though washed at last, still smelled of perfumes used in winter for obvious reasons.

3

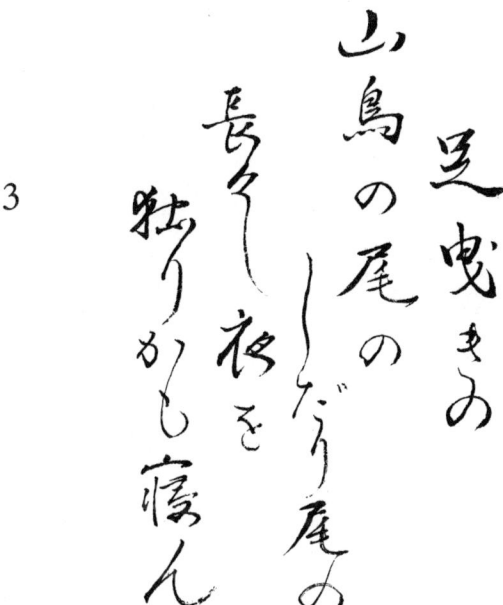

Ashibiki no
Yamadori no o no
　Shidari o no
Naganagashi yo wo
Hitori ka mo nen

　Kakinomoto no Hitomaro
　(d. 708?)

The wild hill pheasants
Drag their feet and drag their tails,
　Splendid though they be,
Through this long, long weary night
Like me, lying here alone.

One of the best, and best known, of the old-time poets, he wrote love songs of a genuineness rarely equaled. This tanka, probably the envoi of a much longer work, was written before the courtiers became too stuffy to use rhythmic repetitions. None of the tenth- and eleventh-century writers would dare end three consecutive lines with the particle *no*. As for those birds, tradition had it that at night each male nested alone.

4

Tago no ura ni
Uchi idete mireba
Shirotae no
Fuji no takane ni
Yuki wa furi tsutsu

Yamabe no Akahito

Pushing and eager,
I run to Little Fields beach
And see a white robe
High on the peak of Fuji
Bold there in the falling snow.

Coming from Nara, he had never seen Fuji, which on his arrival was veiled in mist. Much given to love, as we know from his other poems (though we do not know his dates), he boldly compares the mountain to a lady in her white undergarment *shirotae* (cf. poem 2). From him the expression became so common for "snow-capped" that the average Japanese today would be horrified if told its origin.

5

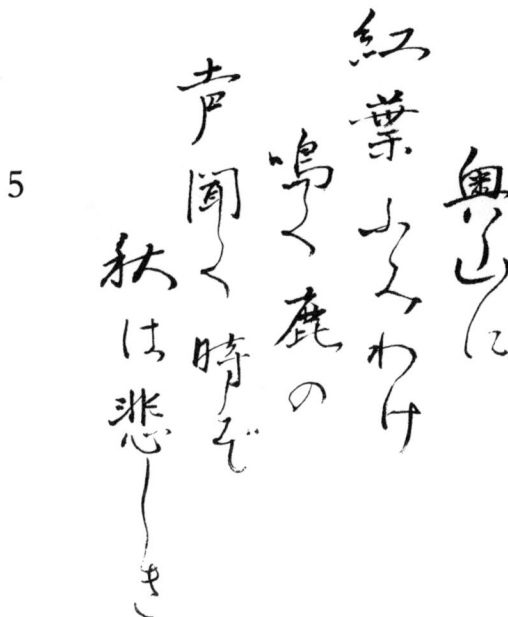

Oku yama ni
Momiji fumiwake
  Naku shiki no
Koe kiku toki zo
Aki wa kanashiki.
  Sarumaru Dayū (fl. 880)

Deep among the hills
Pushing through fallen red leaves
  I have to listen
To the voice of a lone deer
Calling for his mate, also.

Not only does *aki* mean "autumn"; the poet had recently lost his wife Aki. In the famous woodblock print by Hokusai, the loneliness of the place is indicated only by a thatched-roof mountain village, to which, however, even the working women are returning in pairs.

6

Kasasagi no
Wataseru hashi ni
  Oku shimo no
Shiroki wo mireba
Yozo fuke ni keru.

    Ōtomo no Yakamochi (718?-785)

When the magpies' wings
Have joined to let the goddess
  Pass across the sky
If I see them white as frost
This brief night is all but gone.

The *kasasagi* (much like magpies but now extinct) spread their wings to form the Bridge of Heaven, or Milky Way. The festival of the goddess's crossing is now celebrated July 7. In Tokyo in the Imperial Palace grounds an ancient stone bridge is named *Kasasagi no Hashi*, with all these meanings.

7

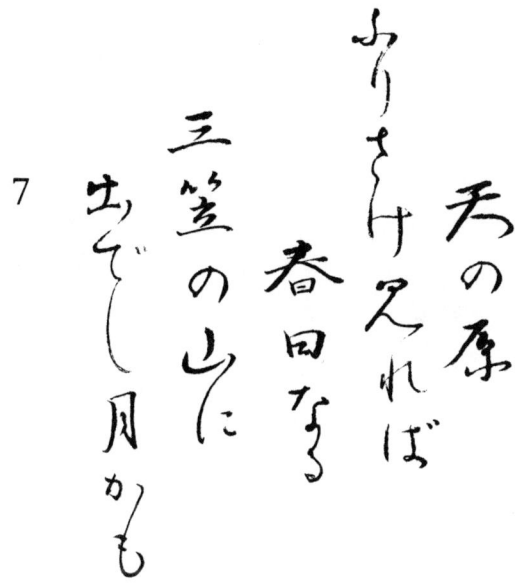

Ama no hara
Furisake mireba
  Kasuga naru
Mikasa no yama ni
Ideshi tsuki kamo

Abe no Nakamaro (701-770)

Once more I regard
The glittering field of sky
  Bright as Day-of-Spring
And ask, near my Three Hats Hill
Has the moon come out, as here?

A study in nostalgia by this ambassador, who, feeling his long stay in China a kind of exile, recalled his native town, Kasuga (Day-of-Spring).

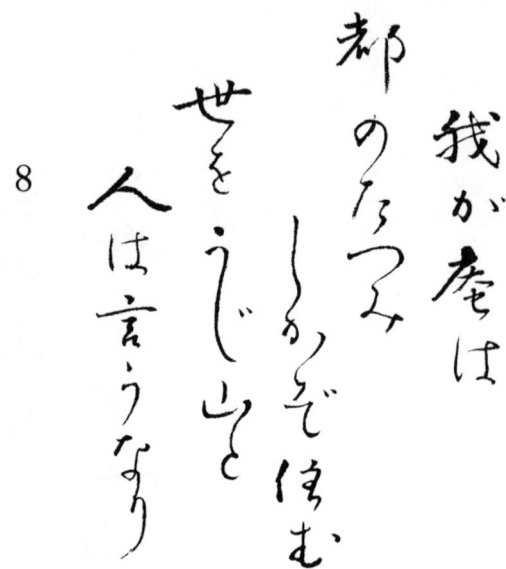

8

Waga iho wa
Miyako no tatsumi
  Shika zo sumu
Yo wo uji yama to
Hito wa iu nari

    The Monk Kisen (early ninth century)

Dreary Hill it's called,
Southeast of the capital;
  Yet here in my hut
I live as peaceful in mind
As the wild deer that I feed.

Once more a sense of humor. He puns on *Uji Yama,* "Royal House Mountain" or "Dreary Hill," and on *shika,* "deer" or "peaceful in mind." (No two editors agree as to what kanji [Chinese characters], or even what kana [Japanese syllable symbols], should be used.)

9

花の色は
移りにけりな
いたずらに
わが身世にふる
ながめせしまに

Hana no iro wa
Utsuri ni keri na
Itazura ni
Waga mi yo ni furu
Nagame seshima ni

Ono no Komachi (mid-ninth century)

See how the blossoms
That are falling about me
Fade after long rain
While, quietly as in prayer,
I have gazed my life away.

Signing herself Komachi, "Small Town," she wrote better poems than the other ladies could. Perhaps they had felt jealous because she had been adopted by the author of poem 11. After his exile her life became difficult.

10

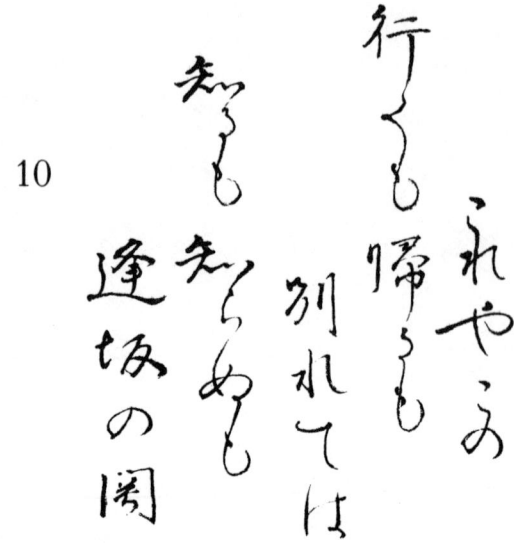

Kore ya kono
Yuku mo kaeru mo
   Wakarete wa
Shiru mo shiranu mo
Ōsaka no seki

   Semimaru (late ninth century)

This is the place where
These coming and those going
   Chat, then separate,
Strangers or friends all the same
Though it's called Meeting Hill Gate.

He was a monk, and one teaching of Buddhism was that though we meet we part; no attachment is permanent, least of all that of a person to this world. (The gate was really so-called because, the roads forming a sort of funnel there, everyone traveling in that district had to come to it.)

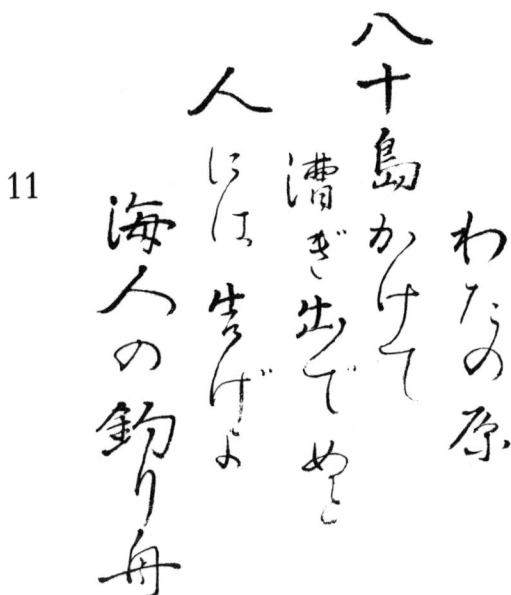

11

Wata no hara
Yaso shima kakete
Kogi idenu to
Hito ni wa tsugeyo
Ama no tsuri bune

Ono no Takamura (802-852)

> O fields of the sea,
> When my ship anchors among
>   The Eighty Islands
> Will that crowd of fishing ships
> Carry the word to my friends?

Exile has been a theme made universal by poets since the most ancient times. The Eighty Islands are a part of the Inland Sea that I photographed repeatedly from a mountaintop as the sun went slowly down, it was so beautiful. Though unable to count them, I noticed that a few were inhabited. The many rocks force the ships into a narrow channel, so that the poet saw a fleet together, as we do.

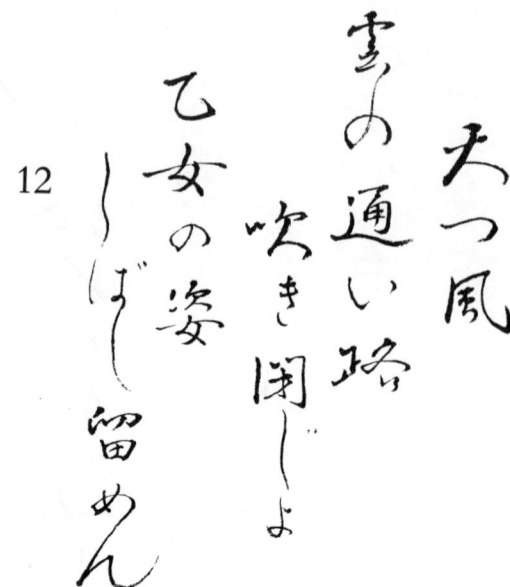

Amatsu kaze
Kumo no kayoiji
Fuki tojiyo
Otome no sugata
Shibashi todomen

　　The Abbot Henjō (816-890)

　　If where clouds travel
　West Wind would bang shut the gate
　　I could watch longer
　The autumn-festival dance
　Of the maidens of heaven.

Having been made a priest for political reasons, this emperor's grandson felt little vocation and, in any case, being athletic, had never wanted to believe the virginity of the Shinto priestesses who danced at court each November third.

13

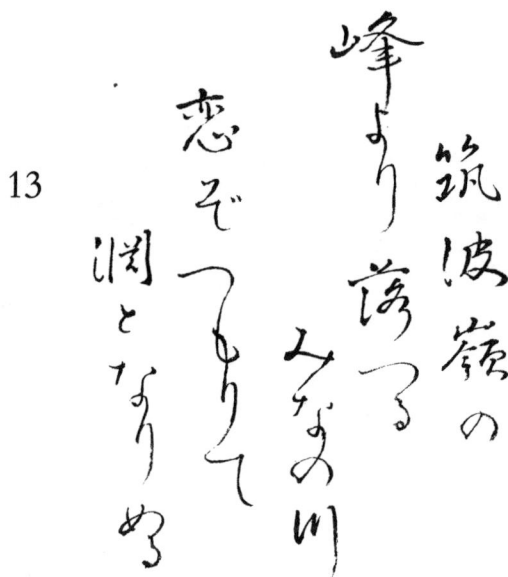

Tsukuba ne no
Mine yori otsuru
Mina no gawa
Koi zo tsumorite
Fuchi to nari nuru

The Retired Emperor Yōzei
(869-949)

Man-Woman River
Leaps from Mt. Tsukuba peak
To the pool below
As our love, once at the heights,
Plunges to become deeper.

This place is considered sacred, perhaps in part because of this poem. It is startling to walk up to the falls and hear human voices from beneath them. I have seen Buddhist devotees sit under the icy shower chanting sutras as an exercise in renunciation. The place-names, including a pun, add mystical overtones: *Mina no gawa*, "Man-Woman River" or "River of Nothingness," falls suicidally (*otsuru*) from Wave-Builder Peak, only to live on as a deep pool leading to the sea, where all things end. Though emperor, he had, for political reasons, been denied the woman he loved. So he walked out on the job.

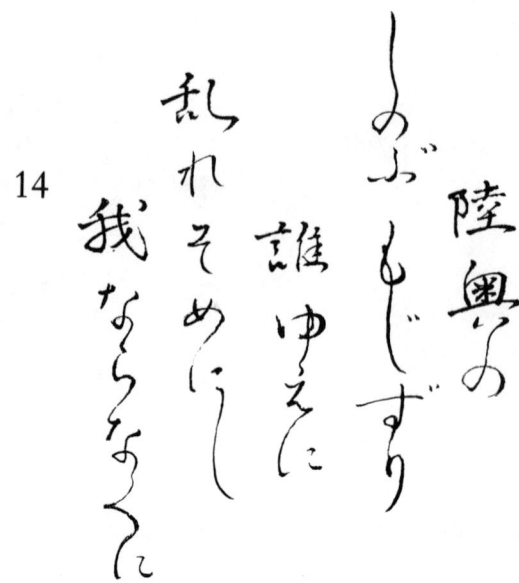

14

Michinoku no
Shinobu moji-zuri
Tare yue ni
Midare some nishi
Ware naranaku ni

Minamoto no Tōru (822-895)

This town is crazy,
Not I, off in this Heart Land,
For in my thoughts you
Guide steadily my footsteps
Where others walk all confused.

His love having accused him of looking at other ladies, this courtier on official business replies with half a dozen puns. For instance, in the town of Shinobu he secretly remembers her (*shinobu*); in the confused streets (*midare*) he is not confused in mind (*midare*); and so on. Can he be serious?

15

Kimi ga tame
Haru no no ni idete
　Wakana tsumu
Waga koromode ni
Yuki wa furi tsutsu

　　Emperor Kōkō (830-887)

　　　　Into the spring fields
　　　I have rushed, seeking our herbs,
　　　　So eager to send
　　　You just this gift, that see how
　　　Snow is falling on my sleeves!

Young princes picked herbs very early in spring, making a party of it, groups of gentlemen and ladies together. To Japanese readers the poem evokes peony-like snowflakes on brocaded sleeves, a beautiful picture.

16

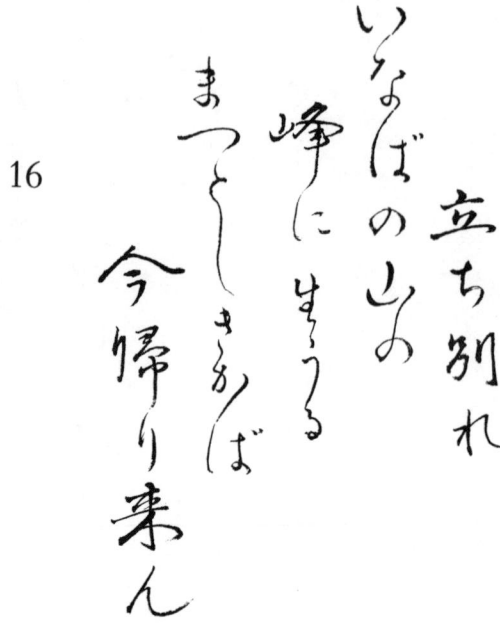

Tachi wakare
Inaba no yama no
  Mine ni ōru
Matsu to shi kikaba
Ima kaeri kon

    Ariwara no Yukihira (818-893)

    Parting in sorrow
    To the heights of Inaba
      Where the old pines grow,
    But I wait for winds to bring
    Your tears; then I will rush back.

This poem so impressed Japanese ears that it was expanded into a famous Noh play, *The Wind in the Pines*. The grammar reveals with touching subtlety that probably the lady will shed no tears, nor he ever return.

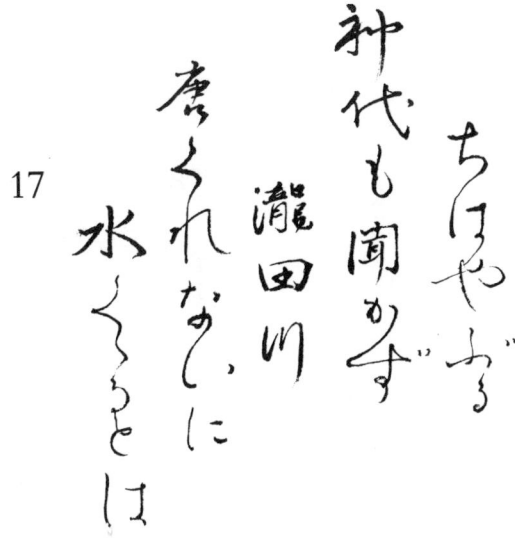

Chiha yaburu
Kami yo mo kikazu
  Tatsuta gawa
Kara kurenaru ni
Mizu kukuru to wa

    Ariwara no Narihira (825-880)

    The thousand islands
Crashed in the era of gods.
  Did you, too, hear them,
Dragon Field River? The red
Autumn enchants your water.

The first two lines, here translated literally, though they have been given many explanations, recall the cataclysms in early mythology told in the Bible, in the Theogony of Hesiod, and in American Indian traditions. *Kukuru* puns on the brilliant red (of maple trees) reflected as though under water or tying it in enchantment.

18

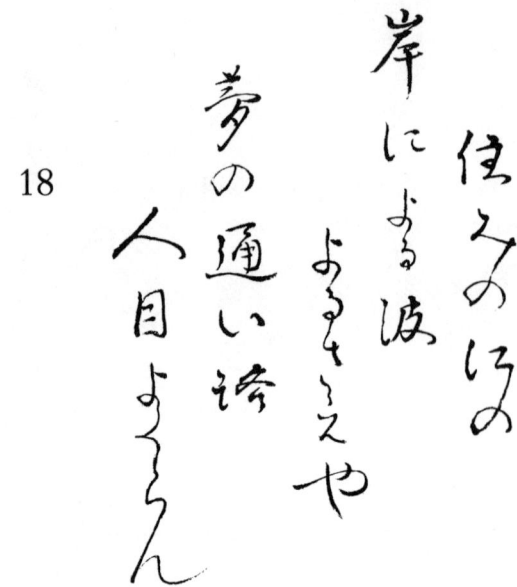

Sumi no e no
Kishi ni yoru nami
  Yoru sae ya
Yume no kayoi ji
Hito me yoku ran

   Fujiwara no Toshiyuki (d. 900?)

      Waves meet openly
    On the shores of Living Bay
        As real people can,
    While I amid my grandeur
    Skulk to you even in dreams.

The modern name, Ōsaka, is a synonym of *kishi* in the poem, "steep shore." The old name was more colorful, *Sumi*, "living." This sort of play on words had become essential in Japanese verse.

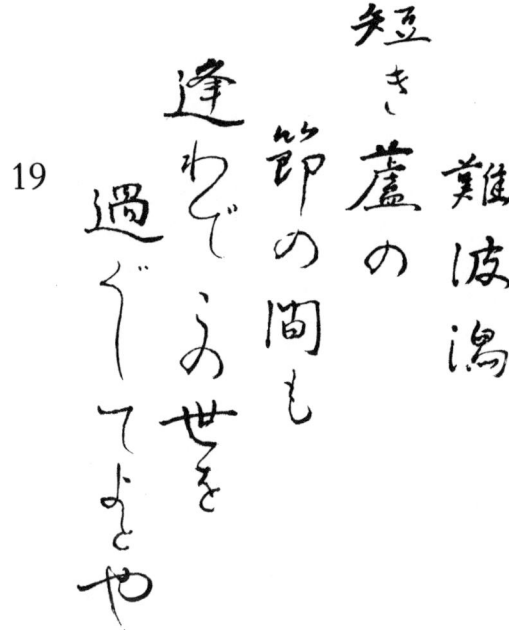

19

Naniwa gata
Mijikaki ashi no
Fushi no ma mo
Awade kono yo wo
Sugu shite yo to ya

Lady Ise (877?-938?)

Do you mean that I
Must trudge my way through this world
 Never with my love
Longer than one reed segment
In Calamity Waves Bay?

Having had a baby by Emperor Uda, she may have felt that she had some rights. She has pretty forcefully made the most of the place-name Naniwa Gata. *Fushi no ma*, space between nodes of a reed, would become a synonym for "a short time."

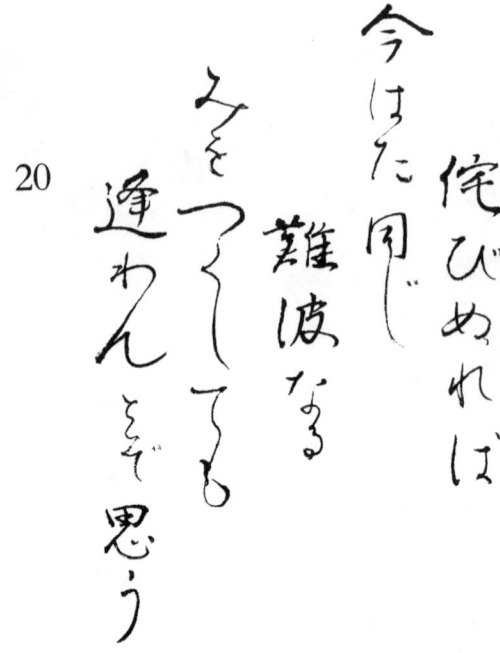

Wabi nureba
Ima hata onaji
  Naniwa naru
Mi wo tsukushite mo
Awan to zo amou

    Prince Motoyoshi (890-943)

What anguish is love!
Now I care not at all though
  Disaster Waves roar;
If only the tide mark stands
I must, I must be with you!

If this crown prince flitted like a butterfly among the ladies, his passion may explain his success.

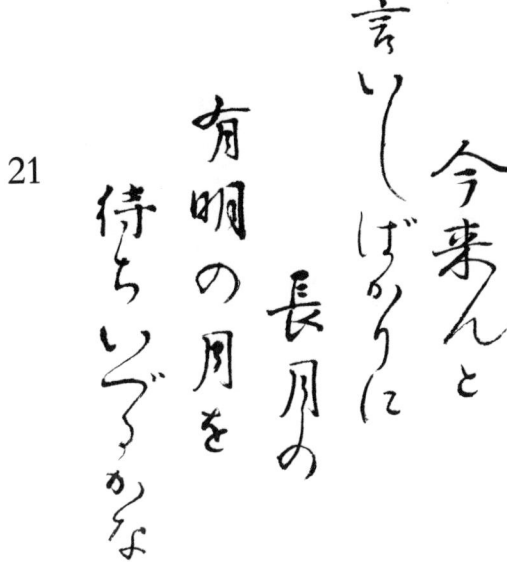

Ima kon to
Iishi bakari ni
Naga tsuki no
Ariake no tsuki wo
Machi izuru kana

The Monk Sosei (late ninth to early tenth century)

The moon is setting
After the long-moon night of
Autumn's end, while I
At dawn still wait to rush out,
For you said now you would come.

By the old system, the last month of autumn, *naga tsuki*, very nearly coincided with our September. *Machi izuru* abbreviates *machidetsuru*, "waiting to go out," for he had expected to rush and meet her. The word was used particularly of fishing boats waiting for the caprices of the weather. She was a little like that. Perhaps he had too many of these disappointments, for he ended as a monk.

22

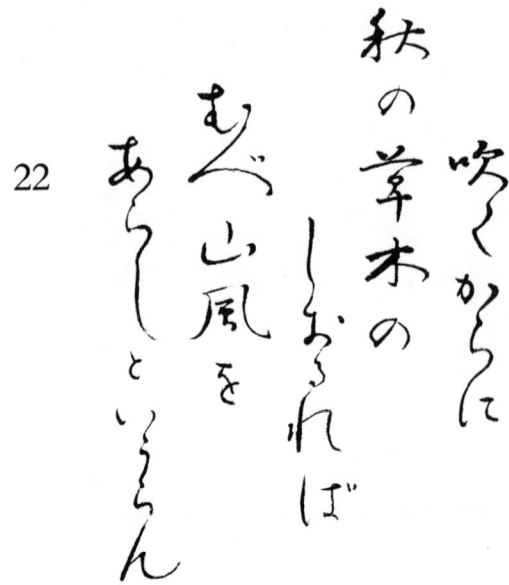

Fuku kara ni
Aki no kusa ki no
  Shiorureba
Mube yama kaze wo
Arashi to iuran

    Funya no Yasuhide (mid-ninth century)

As soon as it blows
From Proper Mountain, the trees
  And autumn grasses
Wither like an aging prince.
It should be named Robber Hill.

The poem is so good, we wish we knew more about the author than that he was one of six famous poets.

23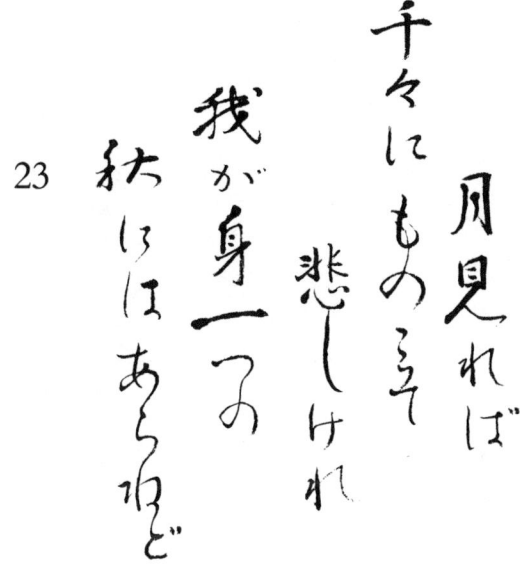

Tsuki mireba
Chiji ni mono koso
Kanashi kere
Waga mi hitotsu no
Aki ni wa aranedo

Ōe no Chisato (late ninth to early tenth century)

When the moon looks down
On our thousands of kinds of
Sadness, this autumn
In the autumn of my life
Comes not to my life only.

From an old Chinese poem, "The moon, which is so cold, looks down on our autumn, just as cold." But the Japanese poet has converted this flat sentiment into a masterpiece by adding the human dimension.

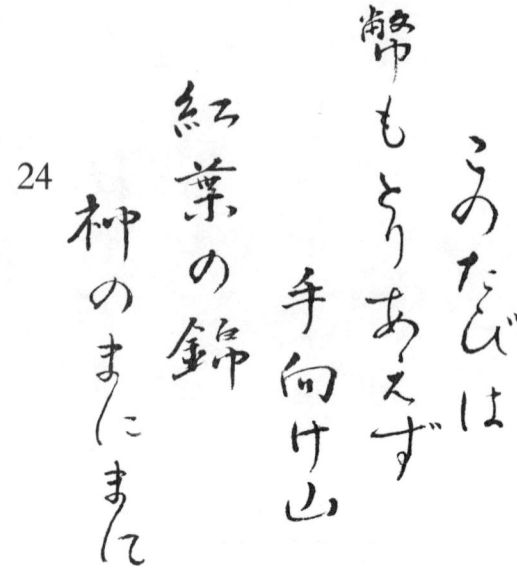

24

Kono tabi wa
Nusa mo tori aezu
Tamuke yama
Momiji no nishiki
Kami no mani mani

Sugawara no Michizane (845-903)

Arriving this time
Brocaded for crown service
  At Thanksgiving Hill,
By the gods' whim what have I
To its garb of maple leaves?

Here the sophisticate's smile conceals the poet's dismay. Suddenly whatever offering he might make in the Shinto shrine at Tamuke Yama would look ridiculous, now that he has wealth, *nusa*. The higher you rise, the harder it is for you to compete with the glories that the gods bestow casually. A poor man's bit of folded paper, *nusa*, would so obviously be more meaningful.

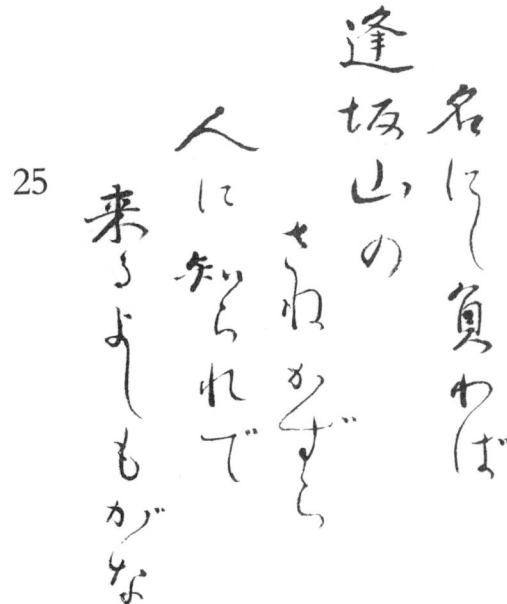

Na ni shi owaba
Ōsaka yama no
　　Sanekazura
Hito ni shirarede
Kuru yoshi mo gana

　　Fujiwara no Sadakata (873-932)

　　　　If it has the name
　　　Berry of sleeping lovers
　　　　　At Meeting Slope Hill,
　　　Surely you will in secret
　　　Come to me and sleep again!

Toying this time with the names of plant and place, the wit has tied his puzzle so intricately that we may never find all its turns. Though this *kazura* may be only a vine with berries that have *sane*, "pits," this word also means "clitoris." Or, again, *sa ne* (two words) is "Let's sleep."

26

小倉山
峰のもみぢ葉
心あらば
今ひとたびの
みゆき待たなん

Ogura yama
Mine no momiji ba
Kokoro araba
Ima hito tabi no
Miyuki matanan

Prince Teishin (880-949)

Maple leaves, maple leaves
On Little Treasury Hill,
Do you have a heart?
Please wait! It won't be long now
Till His Majesty comes here.

Shinto is a nature cult, and the sophisticated poet only partly conceals by his lightness of tone his real belief that what is beautiful is divine and might be moved by sympathy.

27

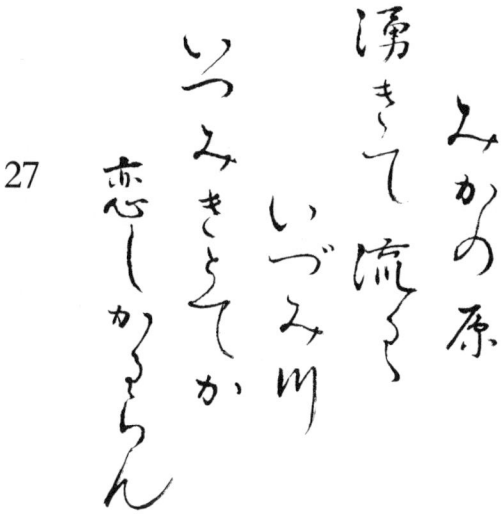

Mika no hara
Wakite nagaruru
Izumi gawa
Itsu mikitote ka
Koishi karuran

Fujiwara no Kanesuke (877-933)

Izumi River
Gushes up for no reason
In a sweet, green field.
Is that like my love for her?
And did I really see her?

The place-names, each with several meanings, are interpreted as the poet wishes. The field of Did I See? and Fountain River both can be translated otherwise. Readers familiar with Petrarch, Laura, and the Fontaine de Vaucluse, where they lived, will recall how a poet can be excited by a river that gushes out of the ground. And it does not take a poet to become dreamy over a woman scarcely seen.

28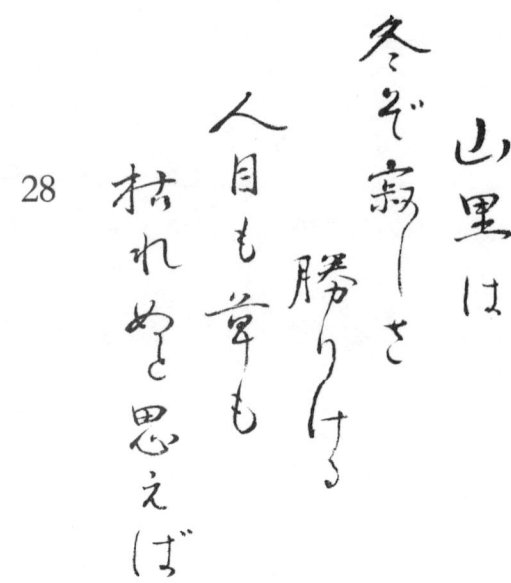

Yama zato wa
Fuyu zo sabishisa
  Masari keru
Hito me mo kusa mo
Karenu to omoeba

  Minamoto no Muneyuki
    (d. 939)

My native hill town
Overdoes this loneliness
  Of winter, when most
People vanish, grass turns brown,
And I, it seems, must wither.

We have seen so many Japanese prints of people traveling in winter, we may forget that, since people did *not* do this, the pictures symbolize misery. The last line, with too many syllables, adds a nuance of absurdity, clearly intentional. The *ba*, grammatically, could be omitted, except that its absence would ruin the poem.

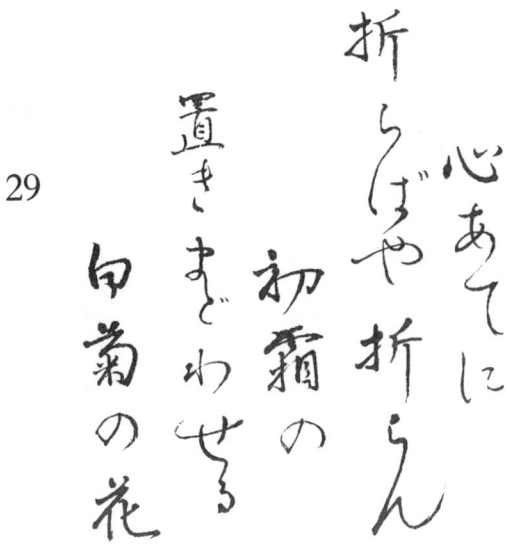

Kokoro ate ni
Orabaya oran
   Hatsu shimo no
Oki madowaseru
Shira giku no hana

<small>Ōshiko-uchi no Mitsune (late ninth to early tenth century)</small>

    Wishing in my heart
    To snip where I used to snip
      White chrysanthemums,
    I stand bewitched. Which are they,
    And which the first autumn frost?

The pun on *oki*, "to put" down his hand to pick a flower or, more commonly, "to put" flowers in the sacred alcove, reveals his purpose. *Madowaseru* is "confused" by white frost and white flowers, or "enchanted" by sunlight on this first beautiful scene of winter. There has been controversy among scholars, who do not at all agree what this poem means.

30

Ariake no
Tsurenaku mieshi
Wakare yori
Akatsuki bakari
Uki mono wa nashi

Mibu no Tadamine (late ninth to early tenth century)

Ever since we saw
How coolly, how heartlessly
Dawn made me leave you,
Even the brightest daybreak
Is to me a thing of grief.

Some translations have interpreted this as saying that she was chilly at parting, but there is nothing about this in the text. Anglo-Saxon men love to bring in a dig now and then against a woman; Japanese regard as unmanly any attempt to shunt troubles off on her.

31

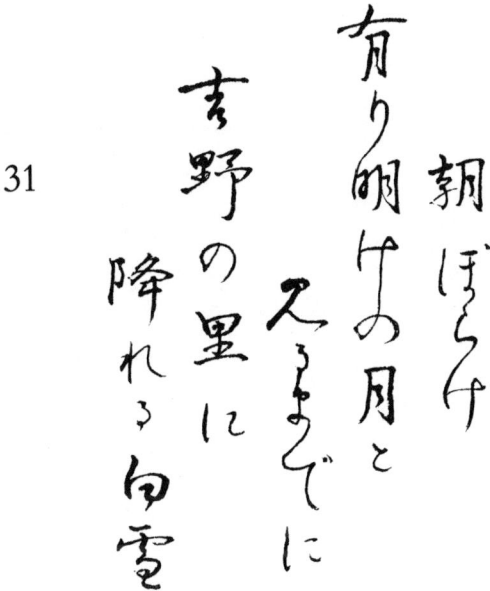

Asaborake
Ariake no tsuki to
  Miru made ni
Yoshino no sato ni
Fureru shira yuki

<small>Saka-no-ue no Korenori (late ninth to early tenth century)</small>

Just before daybreak
Moonlight made everything white
  Till at last I saw
Over Happy Fields Village
The sifting small white snowflakes.

Of all the ways to describe Nara, the poet has chosen the most appropriate, for it was a town in Yoshino (Happy Fields) district. For modern ears the poem has a cheerful confusion, since *Yoshino-gama* has come to mean white tissue paper used as artificial snow. *Sato*, "village," does not mean that Nara was really small, but that it was right out in the country.

32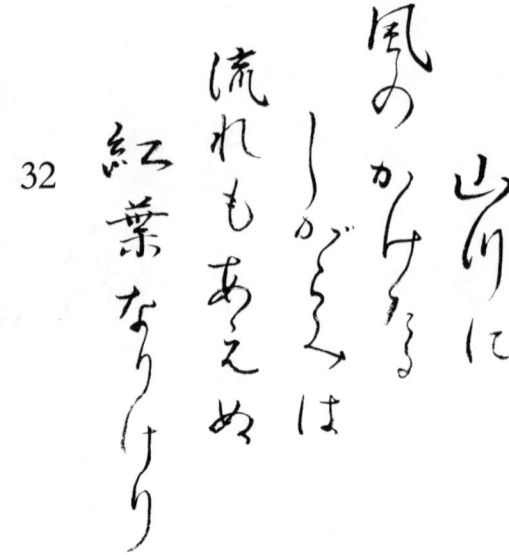

Yama gawa ni
Kaze no kaketaru
  Shigarami wa
Nagare mo aenu
Momiji nari keri

    Harumichi no Tsuraki (d. 920)

    Playing in the stream,
The wind like a busy child
  Has set up a dam
That blocks the mountain torrent
With a glory of bright leaves.

The poet saw this at Mt. Hie on the slope toward Lake Biwa. Some of these words later acquired different meanings, but *kaketaru* usually meant a child at play. Now at maple-viewing season the National Railroad schedules special trains to such places.

33

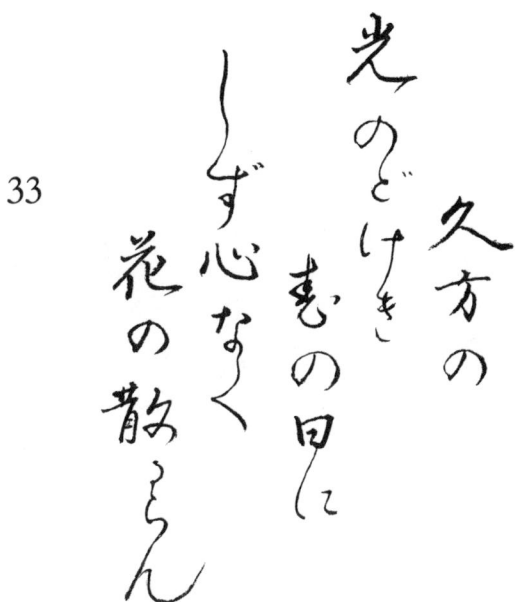

Hisakata no
Hikari nodokeki
  Haru no hi ni
Shizu kokoro naku
Hana no chiruran

  Ki no Tomonori (fl. ca. 905)

      Long, for a long time
      The days of spring pour on us
        Their unchanging light.
      Can they not give peace of mind?
      Now the petals are falling.

This is the picture that we find in *The Tale of Genji*, elegance and refined pleasure everywhere, in a social structure that makes no one happy. *Hisakata*, "a long time," "the whole sky," or "heaven's mysteries," which are responsible for all this, adds a theological nuance not spelled out.

34

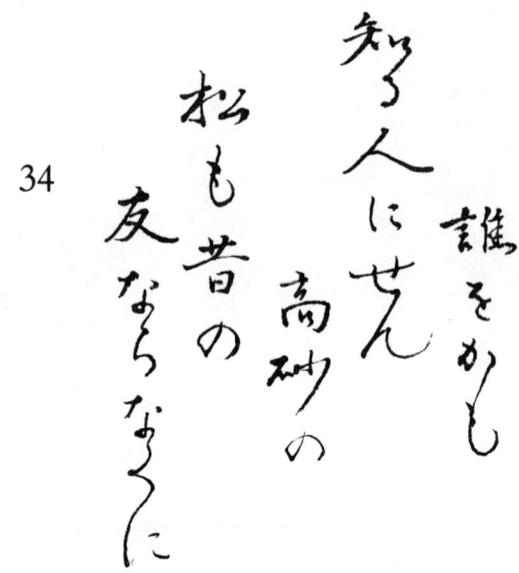

Tare wo kamo
Shiru hito ni sen
  Takasago no
Matsu mo mukashi no
Tomo nara naku ni

Fujiwara no Okikaze (late ninth to mid-tenth century)

With whom should I here
Go bidding for acquaintance?
  Even the pine trees
That have stood from ancient times
On High Sand are not friendly.

This poet has gone rather far with a place-name, asking, How could a town called Takasago (High Sand) hold any but dry, gritty people? In these last two or three poems the sound patterns begin to be more important than what is said.

35

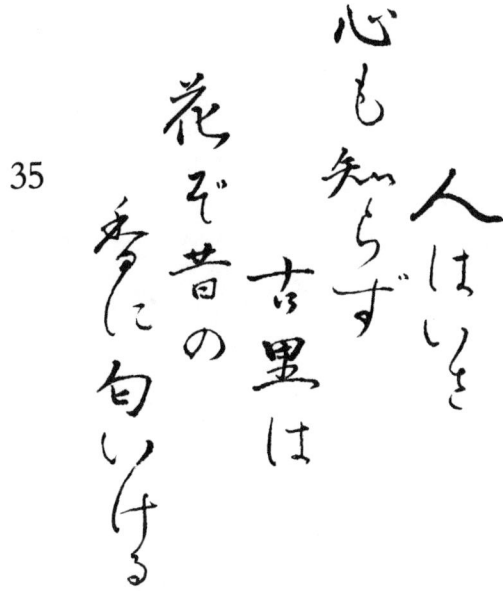

Hito wa isa
Kokoro mo shirazu
Furu sato wa
Hana zo mukashi no
Ka ni nioi keru

Ki no Tsurayuki (868?-945?)

I cannot well know
What human feelings may do,
But in this village
The plum blossoms anyway
Still have the fragrance of old.

After long absence the poet returned to his native village, which was as well known for its plum blossoms as he for his verses to ladies. He sent this tanka ahead to one whom he had not seen since youth. Courteously he avoids personal reference by writing simple statements of large meaning. The rest is up to her.

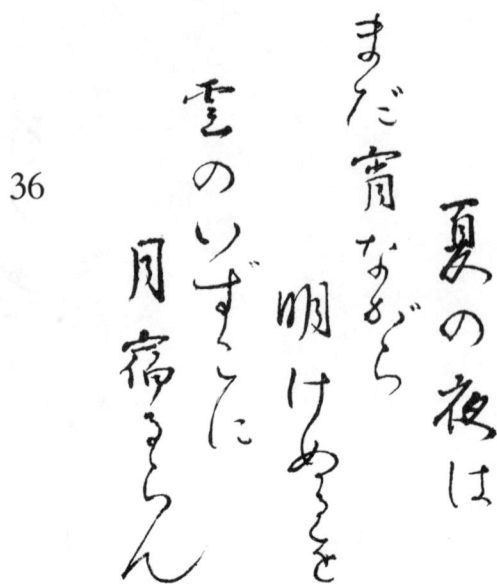

*Natsu no yo wa
Mada yoi nagara
　Akenuru wo
Kumo no izuko ni
Tsuki yado ruran*

<small>Kiyohara no Fukayabu (late ninth to early tenth century)</small>

　Little summer night,
Scarcely has twilight ended
　When dawn rushes in.
Where so soon among the clouds
Can Moon find a place to sleep?

Again a sophisticated poet conceals under a light manner the depth of his feeling about the transience of love and perhaps of human life also.

37

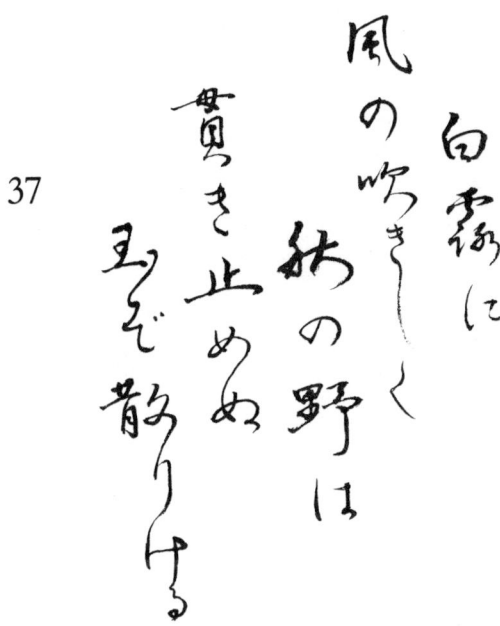

Shira tsuyu ni
Kaze no fukishiku
Aki no no wa
Tsuranuki tomenu
Tama zo chiri keru

Funya no Asayasu (late ninth to early tenth century)

Every rush of wind
Scatters across the stubble
Glistening white dewdrops
Like strings of pearls come untied
That tumble from ladies' hair.

Chinese opera and some Japanese geisha preserve these ancient ornaments, which dangle in clusters from comb or large hairpin. The sound pattern here is particularly subtle and suited to the pearls (the text says only "pierced jewels"). It begins and ends with *shira, chiri*. First line, *ra tsu*; fourth, *tsura*; fifth, this is compressed to *ta*. In successive lines: *uki, iku, aki, uki*. And so on.

38

Wasuraruru
Mi wo ba omowazu
  Chikaite shi
Hito no inochi no
Oshiku mo aru kana

    Lady Ukon (mid-tenth century)

It does not matter
That I am now forgotten,
  But making an oath
Is the most precious moment
In the whole life of a man.

This poem is unique in the collection, wholly abstract, with not one image. It is redeemed and loved because of the greatness expressed. Wisely the Emperor Daigo chose this woman to share the throne with him, and she is remembered, her foresworn lover forgotten.

    An alternate reading of the last line—*shaku mo aru kana*—would immensely improve the poem but might not be accepted by some scholars.

39

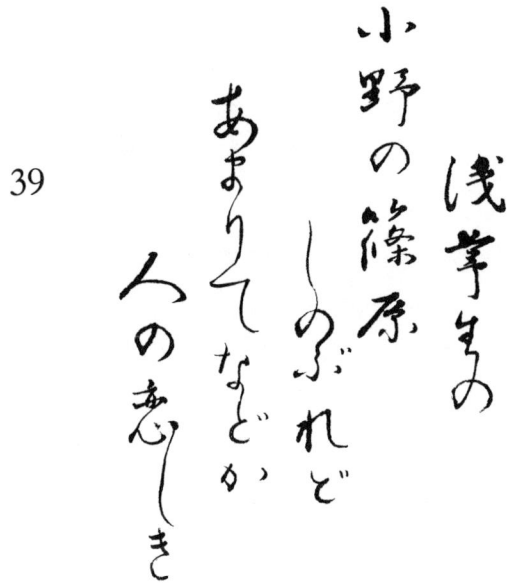

Asajifu no
Ono no shinohara
　Shinoburedo
Amarite nado ka
Hito no koishiki

Minamoto no Hitoshi (880-951)

The tough bamboo-weed
And the soft pussy willow
Grow again when cut.
Why is love of a lady
More than a man can endure?

The shrewd anthologist has immediately returned us to a poem crammed with images and puns: e.g., *shino*, "bamboo-weed"; *shinobu*, "to endure." An alternate reading of the first line—*Asa ji ono*—would make the involution really marvelous.

　As with most desperate love songs, we do not know how serious this is, but it has the merit of universality. How many millions of poets have shouted, "I'll die if I don't get that girl!"

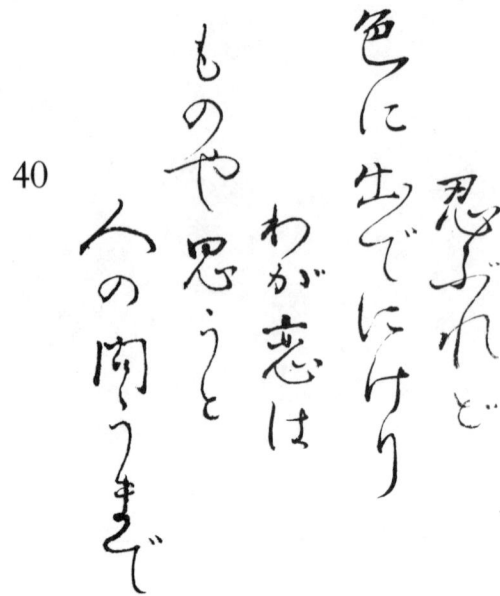

Shinoburedo
Iro ni ide ni keri
  Waga koi wa
Mono ya omou to
Hito no tou made

Taira no Kanemori (d. 990)

It has been hidden;
Yet the color that bursts out
  When love is endured
Leads people into asking,
"Have you something on your mind?"

With its puns running all one way—*shinoburu*, "to hide" or "to endure"; *iro*, "color" or "love" (or "lust")—this passion poem resembles British understatement. *Mono ya omou* should almost be read with an Eton accent.

41

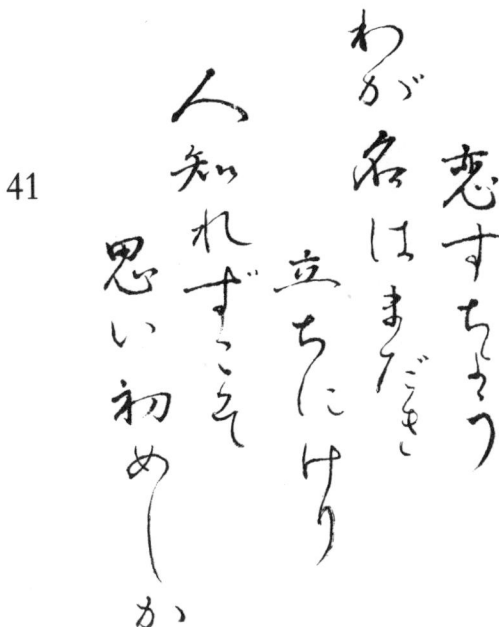

Koi su chō
Waga na wa madaki
Tachi ni keri
Hito shirezu koso
Omoi someshi ka

Mibu no Tadami (mid-tenth century)

As yet a bit young
For a real name as lover
To be established,
I've begun these thoughts of you,
People indeed not knowing.

The amorous reputation of this poet's father (author of poem 30) caused the son to be both watched and wary. This apparently open avowal is so subtle that everyone disputes its meaning. The first three lines are quoted in full in a dictionary of old Japanese, which insists that *madaki* does not mean "early morning" (because some scholars say it does). And so on.

42

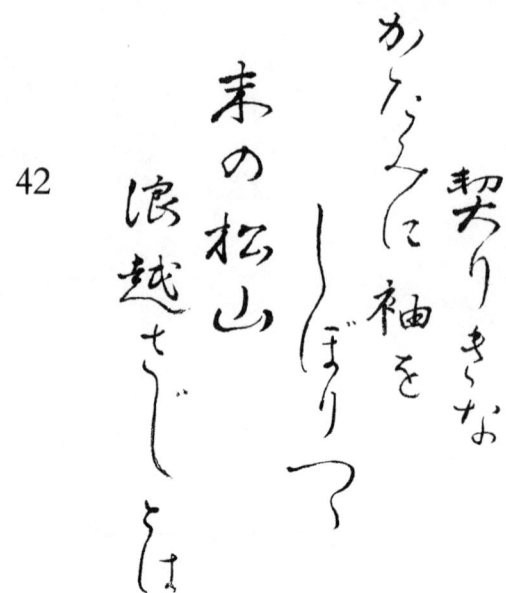

Chigiriki na
Katami ni sode wo
  Shibori tsutsu
Sue no matsu yama
Nami kosaji to wa

  Kiyohara no Motosuke (908-990)

We may soak our sleeves
With tears for one another;
  Yet our promise holds
Till Pine Mountain in Sue
Shall be erased by the waves.

Though Sue is a place-name, *sue no* also means "to the very end" (future tense). This is one of several poems in this collection that make one shake one's head over our classicists' notion that oriental poets never burst out with emotion.

43

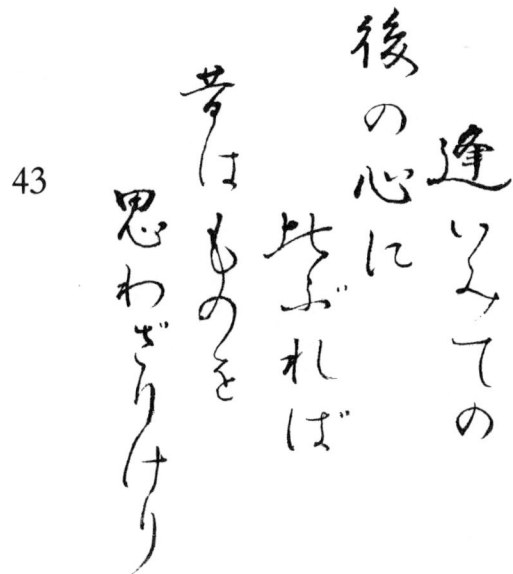

Ai mite no
Nochi no kokoro ni
  Kurabureba
Mukashi wa mono wo
Omowazari keri

Fujiwara no Atsutada (904-943)

If I but compare
All that I find in my heart
  Since one night with her,
What had I there formerly
But peace—yes—and nothingness?

Again a controversial poem, here translated literally, line by line. Devotees of American Zen have seen in that "nothingness" their Nirvana, better of course than a mere woman—ignoring the detail that the poet lived three hundred years before Zen came to Japan.

44

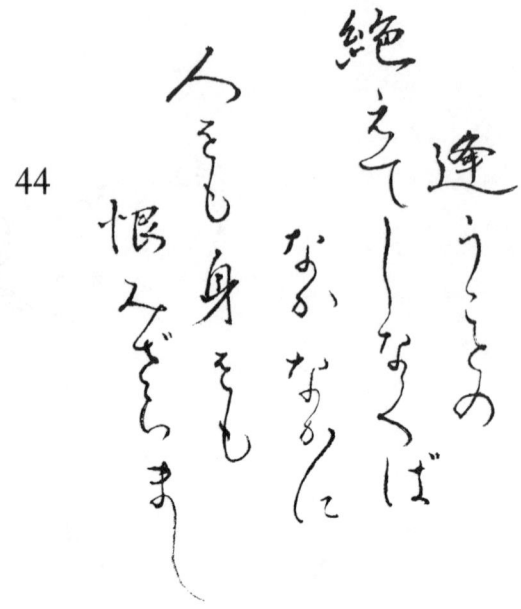

Au koto no
Taete shi nakuba
Naka naka ni
Hito wo mo mi wo mo
Uramizarama shi

Fujiwara no Asatada (910-966)

Now, if making love
Were just an extinct custom,
Neither to oneself
Nor to the lady would come
These heavy hours of regret.

The debonair good humor in the second line, *Taete shinakuba*, "if it would just become extinct," bars out the discourteous interpretation sometimes given to this poem. Despite all similarities to the previous tanka, the poets were only distant cousins.

45

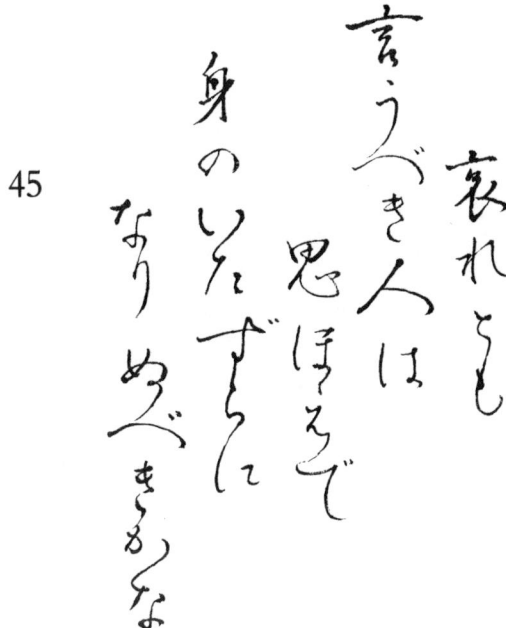

Aware to mo
Iu beki hito wa
  Omohoede
Mi no itazura ni
Narinu beki kana

Prince Kentoku (914-972)

    She might even say
—Yes, of me—"What a pity!"
    Yet deep in her heart
Would she be considering
That I waste away for her?

Again a difficult poem, which I have untangled by translating literally, line by line. *Hito* at that time commonly meant "she." However, since he rose to power in the cabinet and lived to be fifty-eight, we shall risk supposing that being abandoned by a lady, though hard enough, was not lethal rapidly.

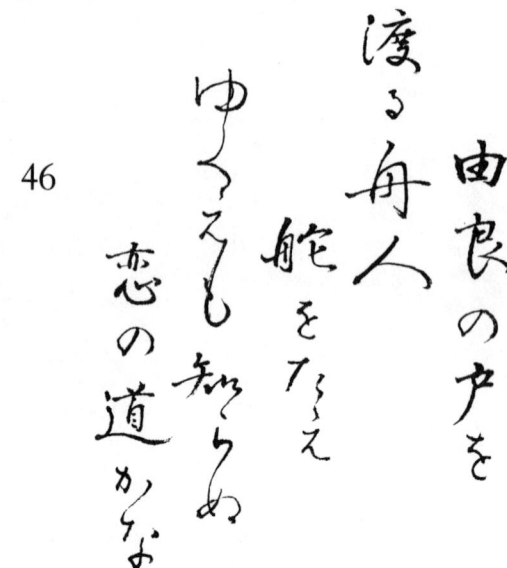

46

Yura no to wo
Wataru funabito
   Kaji wo tae
Yukue mo shiranu
Koi no michi kana

     Sone no Yoshitada (tenth century)

Suppose some boatmen
Sailing into Yura Straits
   Have lost their rudder.
They will be no more at sea
Than I on the path of love.

The place-name could not be more apt: The Straits of Good Reason.

47

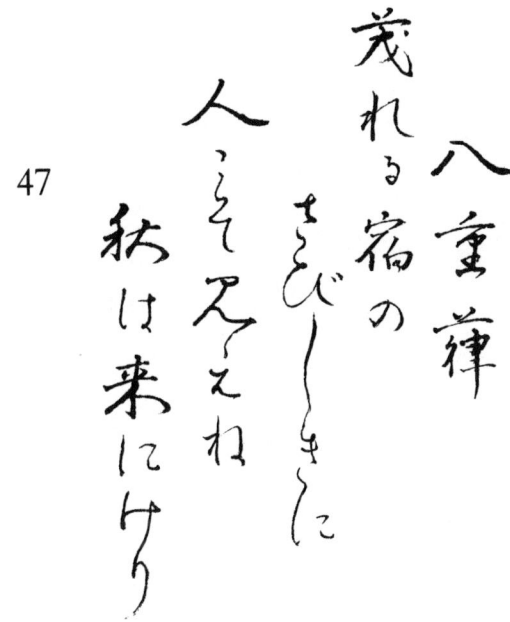

Yaemugura
Shigereru yado no
Sabishiki ni
Hito koso miene
Aki wa ki ni keri

The Monk Egyō (late tenth century)

Eight-layer goose grass
Thrives, rampant, about my house
In this remote place
Where in weeks no one is seen,
Yet the autumn winds arrive.

Since this poem, the phrase "goose-grass house" has become a synonym for "humble hut." The odd adjective, by the bye, is rendered "double-petaled" in English, but is more accurate in Japanese, as the clustered petals never are merely double. To a monk, *hito* was not "she" but "people."

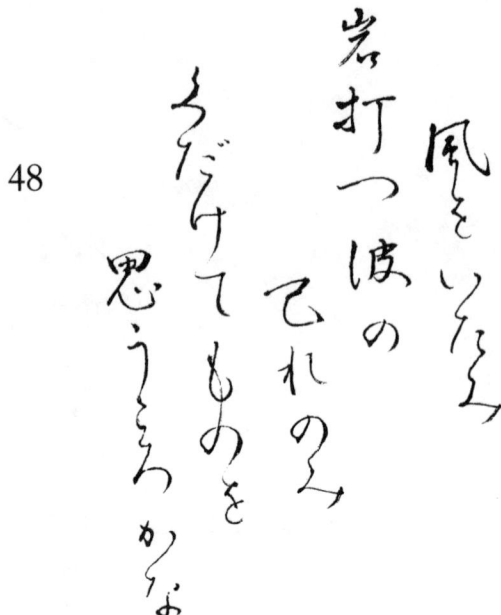

Kaze wo itami
Iwa utsu nami no
Onore nomi
Kudakete mono wo
Omou koro kana

<small>Minamoto no Shigeyuki (tenth century)</small>

What makes the wind moan
Is only myself crashing
  In waves on the reef.
Alas! Do you one moment
Ponder what is breaking here?

After trying various flat paraphrases, I resorted to this word-for-word rendering, which, I must say, startled me. *Itami* can mean "to pain" or "to moan." The sound pattern is particularly musical. The poem begins and ends with *kaze, kana*. We notice *itami, nami, mi no, nomi, mono,* and so forth. Since it is a syllabic language, the poets tend to think in terms of *mi, ka, no* . . . not individual sounds.

49

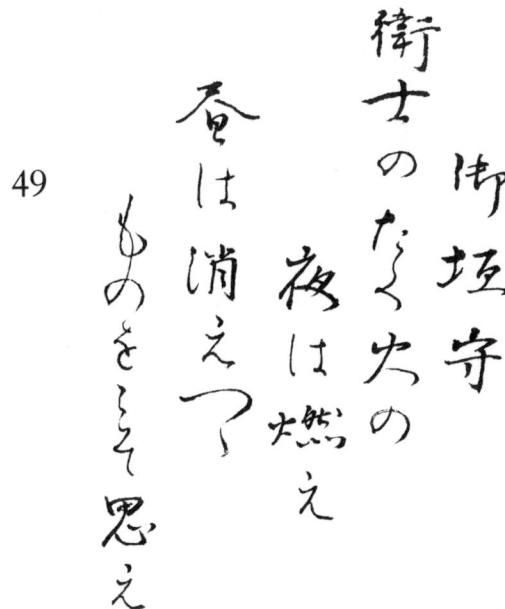

Mikaki mori
Eji no taku hi no
  Yoru wa moe
Hiru wa kie tsutsu
Mono wo koso omoe

    Ōnakatomi no Yoshinobu (911-991)

Why speak of me now
When His Majesty sees you?
   The guardsmen build fires
That dusk ignites and high noon
Extinguishes. You know that.

Only this minister of the high, inner cabinet had the nerve for such a poem. The elegantly constructed gem glitters smoothly till we are jolted by the sharp last line.

50

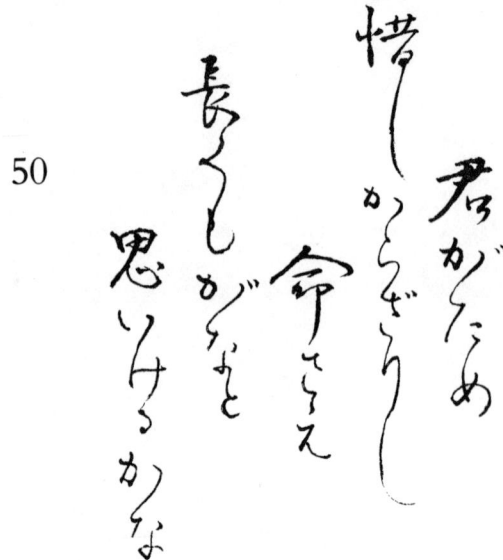

Kimi ga tame
Oshi kara zarishi
   Inochi sae
Nagaku mogana to
Omoi keru kana

Fujiwara no Yoshitaka (954-974)

Now because of you,
After feeling that my life
   Was but tiresome time,
I begin at last to wish
That it may be very long.

There but for modern medicine go plenty of us. With penicillin and the encouragement of that girl he might have made it; his dates reveal that he had not a chance.

51

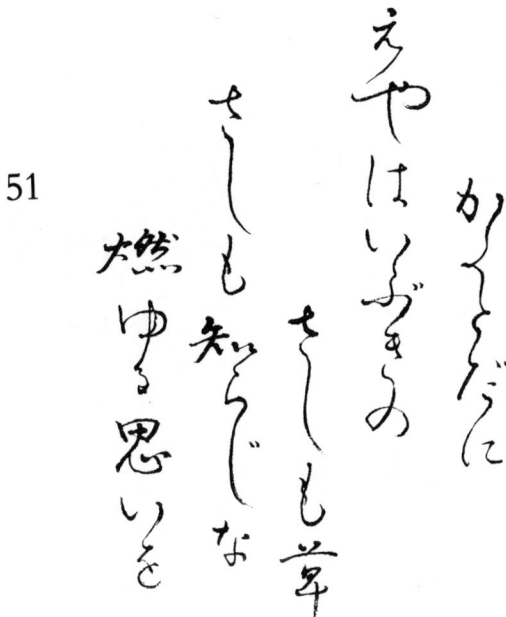

Kaku to dani
Eyawa ibuki no
  Sashi mogusa
Sashimo shiraji na
Moyuru omoi wo

Fujiwara no Sanekata (d. 998)

    Sashimogusa
Is a flower that blooms like fire
  On I-Cannot-Tell.
How can I tell, or you know,
What burns in me now? Alas!

What a contrast to the previous writer!

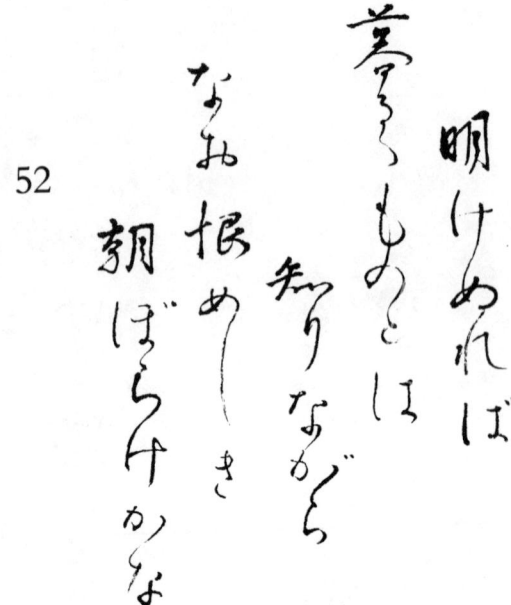

Akenureba
Kururu mono to wa
  Shiri nagara
Nao urameshiki
Asaborake kana

    Fujiwara no Michinobu (972-994)

When the dawn parts us
Darkness to come is something
  I ought to believe;
Yet in bitterness of heart
Each day I see sweet sunlight.

Though such a poem suggests a secret love affair, we are told that in those days in elegant circles a young husband lived with his own family, going to his wife only at night. As he grew older, and especially if his father died, he assembled his own family, as in the next poem.

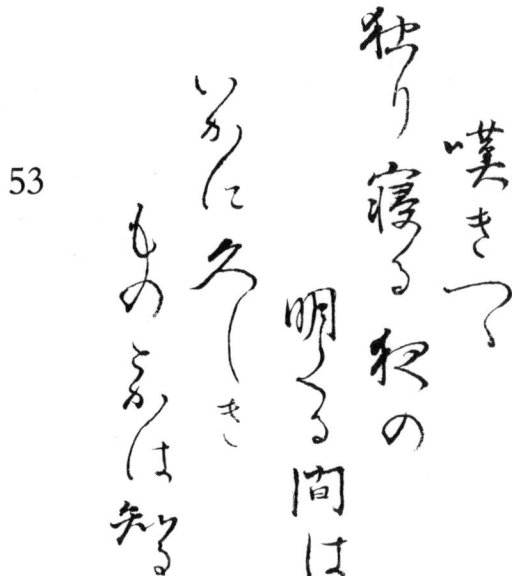

53

Nageki tsutsu
Hitori nuru yo no
   Akuru ma wa
Ikani hisashiki
Mono to kawa shiru

The Mother of Michitsuna (937-995)

Sighing and weeping,
Waiting for the light of dawn
   As one lies alone,
Have you ever thought at all
About how long this can seem?

While she was young enough to worry about her husband's affairs, and her son was still a baby, she one night locked the gate; next morning the husband knocked outside, and she angrily threw this over to him. Her forceful character may explain her son, a famous army commander.

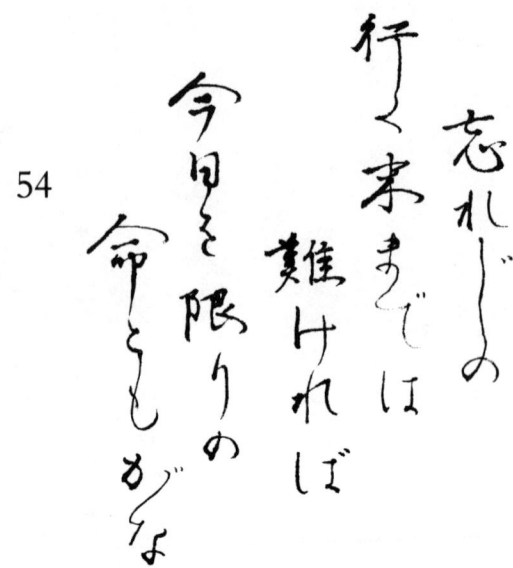

Wasureji no
Yukusue made wa
  Katakereba
Kyō wo kagiri no
Inochi tomo gana

<small>Takako, Mother of Gidō Sanshi (d. 996)</small>

    Not to desert me
Even to the very end,
    As you have told me—
Should that wish prove difficult,
Rather let life end today.

This parallels the Irish legend of Deirdre, who would have nothing less than perfection, else she chose death. If there is any chance of my losing you later on, let's not enjoy today!

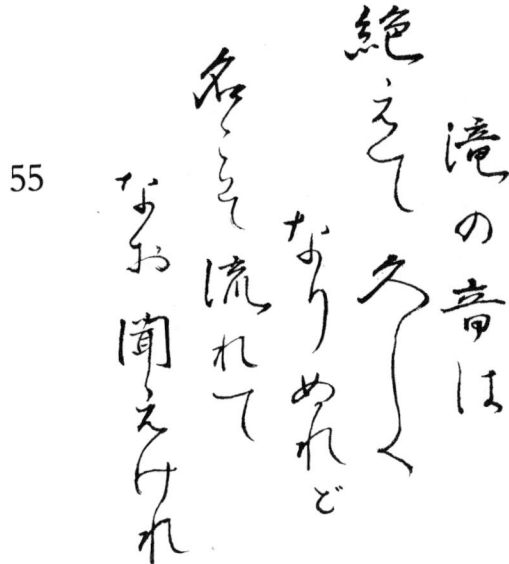

Taki no oto wa
Taete hisashiku
  Narinuredo
Na koso nagarete
Nao kikoe kere

    Fujiwara no Kintō (966-1041)

    Though we hear that the
    Dragon of the waterfall
      Has long been unheard,
    Still that fellow will keep on
    Rumbling in our flow of talk.

Here we see at once that we are in the later, clever period. The poem has stuck in memory by its wit (though the waterfall has ceased to fall, its fame flows on) and by its sonal involutions (*taki, taete; na . . . re, nako . . . re . . . na . . . ko . . . re*), which, though not very musical, contribute to the fun.

56

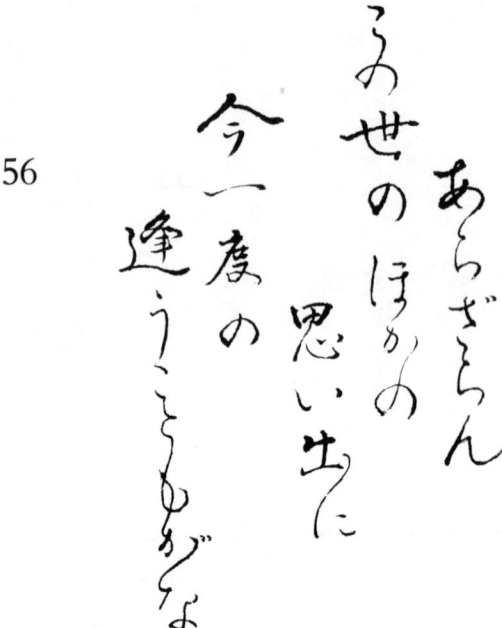

Arazaran
Kono yo no hoka no
  Omoide ni
Ima hito tabi no
Au koto mo gana

    Lady Izumi Shikibu (fl. ca. 1000)

In the thought that soon
Outside this world I shall be
  Where there is nothing,
If only I could see you
And speak with you once again!

Here, with the author of the last part of *The Tale of Genji*, we return to sincerity, a much simpler sonal pattern, and real musicality. Translators having given this poem meanings quite opposite to one another, I have kept this literal, word for word.

Meguri aite
Mishi ya sore tomo
Wakanu ma ni
Kumogakure nishi
Yowa no tsuki kana

> Lady Murasaki Shikibu
> (978?-1016)

Could I distinguish
When I went there to meet him
Whether it was he?
He passed by, as at midnight
The moon slid away in clouds.

This being by the author of *The Tale of Genji*, the sonal effects are, of course, far subtler than in the others. Also the verse conveys that novelist's well-known nuance of reserve. Seeing again a man who had been a playmate in childhood, she, with her storyteller's interest in people, looked eagerly. But he vanished like the midnight moon.

58

有馬山
猪名の笹原
風吹けば
いでそよ人を
忘れやはする

Arima yama
Ina no sasawara
Kaze fukeba
Ide soyo hito wo
Wasure yawa suru

Lady Katako (b. 999)

As the wind prances
Frolicking the cattail leaves
Under Our-Horse Hill,
You rush to this love or that,
But how can I forget you?

Sasawara, which we do not have, resembles our cattails and grew tall near a river. Since this poem the expression "He acts like the wind" has meant "He is changeable." The author was a daughter of the novelist of the previous poem.

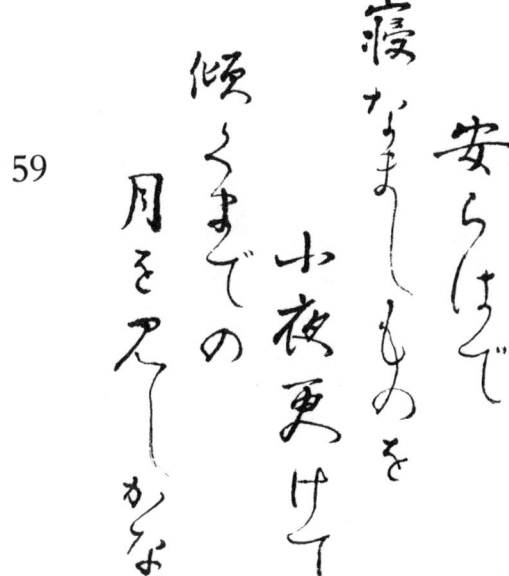

Yasurawade
Nenamashi mono wo
Sayo fukete
Katabuku made no
Tsuki wo mishi kana

Lady Akazome Emon (late ninth to early tenth century)

Not troubling myself
I should have just gone to sleep
As the evening went
Into night. Instead I wait
And see the moon tip downward.

Discreetly, she does not say straight out that he had promised to visit her that night.

60

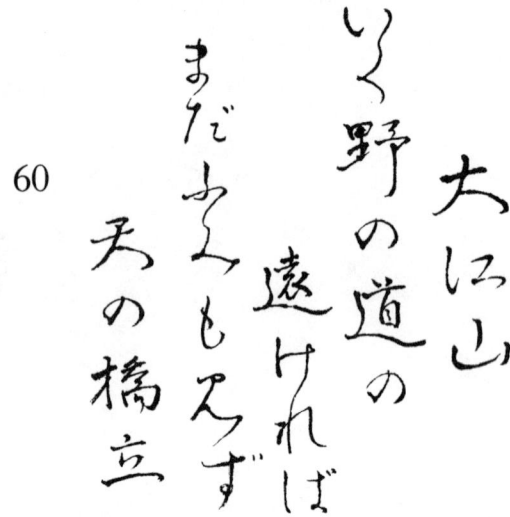

Ōe yama
Ikuno no michi no
　Tō kereba
Mada fumi mo mizu
Ama no hashidate

　　　Lady Koshikibu (1000?-1025)

Though I have come far
Over Big Inlet Hill and
　The field called Living,
I have not even stepped on
Your scripts or Milky Way shore.

Arriving at a formal poets' convention, where each knelt on a separate tatami mat, this daughter of Lady Izumi (poem 56) was at once told, "It is your turn." So she improvised on immediate things. Fully exploiting local place-names, she delighted her audience with two puns: *iku*, "going" or "living"; and *fumi*, "writings" or "step on." The poem also expresses her annoyance at being called on when still out of breath.

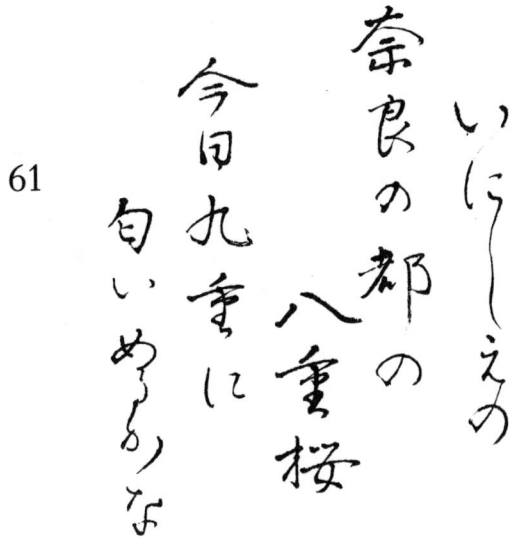

61

Inishie no
Nara no miyako no
  Yae-zakura
Kyō kokonoe ni
Nioi nuru kana

    Lady Ise no Taifu *(early eleventh century)*

So much has left us!
Yet in ancient Nara bloom
  Eight-petaled cherries
On the nine-leaved palace grounds
Still just as fragrant today.

The Nara palace (abandoned capital) may or may not have had nine sections; it was so named for one in China that did. And the cherries even today are a special variety. Since *Nara,* besides being a name, also meant either "good remedy" or "always reliable," the poet felt nostalgic in more ways than one.

62

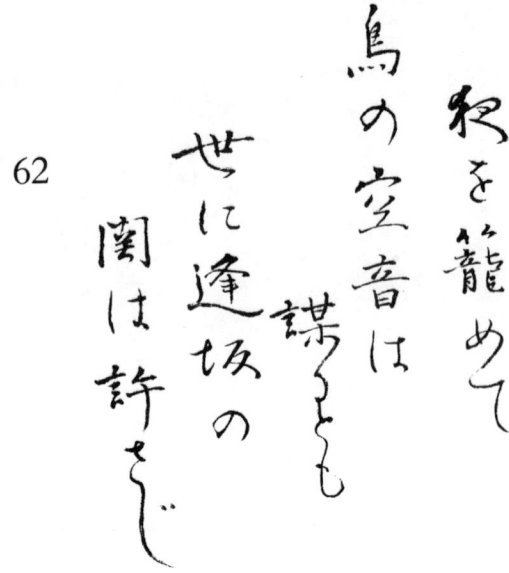

Yo wo komete
Tori no sorane wa
　Hakaru tomo
Yo ni ōsaka no
Seki wa yurusaji

　　Lady Sei Shōnagon (966?-after 1017)

　　You may try that trick
　　Of imitating cockcrow
　　　In the dark of night,
　　But never will this guardsman
　　At Meeting Pass let you pass.

Having read Chinese books, as other ladies did not, this blunt, forthright author of *The Pillow Book* refers to an old story. The Tang ambassador, in a hurry, came to a barrier that would not open till cockcrow. Though still in darkness, he imitated a rooster, the gates opened, and he was admitted. (And the Tangs won the war, of course.) But you, silly boy, do you think I will let you in like a Tang ambassador? For dissimulation she brings in the famous barrier referred to in poem 10.

63

Ima wa tada
Omoi taenan
To bakari wo
Hito zute narade
Iu yoshi mo gana

<small>Sakyō no Daibu Michimasa
(993-1054)</small>

Now when forever
You must be hidden from us
May I not, rather
Than send these mere messengers,
Speak one word to you? Alas!

The lady he loved was a daughter of Emperor Sanjō, who gave her to serve at the Ise Shrine and put guards around her to keep her suitor away. In how many cultures and times and religions has this same barbarous idealism been familiar? And this poet was only *Daibu*, "courtier of the fifth rank." That would not do at all.

64

Asaborake
Uji no kawagiri
　Tae dae ni
Araware wataru
Seze no ajiro-gi

Fujiwara no Sadayori
(995-1045)

　　　　It is early dawn,
　　And across Uji River
　　　　Dimly through the fog
　　The fish weirs are unspeaking
　　Robed ghosts who ford the shallows.

Again a poem in which the pattern of sounds, unusual and subtle, is almost more important than what is said. The place-name, Uji ("home guards"), suggests who the intermittently seen ghosts may be.

65

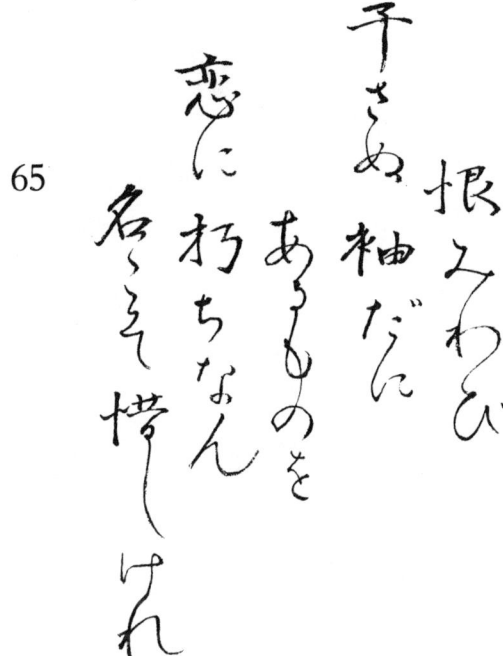

Urami wabi
Hosanu sode da ni
Aru mono wo
Koi ni kuchinan
Na koso oshikere

Lady Sagami (998?-1068?)

When love turns to spite,
Sleeves are dampened in anguish;
Yet one thing still is
Worse than wilting, forgotten:
That is, being talked about.

The story is that, finding him at a poets' meeting, she handed this tanka to him to read aloud. After so much courtesy, we are startled by the blunt, almost violent language here.

66

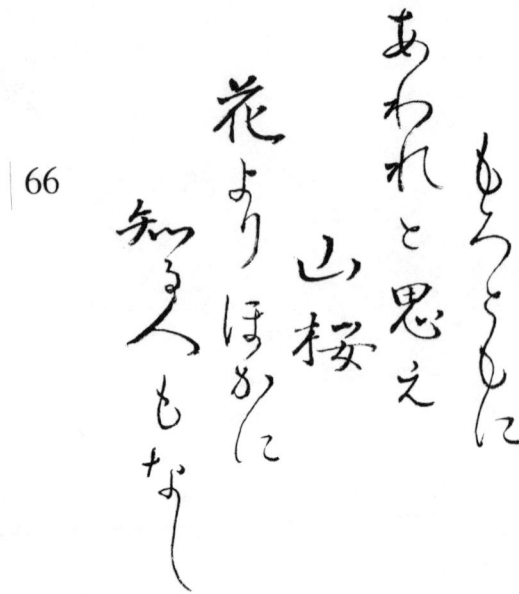

Morotomo ni
Aware to omoe
Yama-zakura
Hana yori hoka ni
Shiru hito mo nashi

    Former Chief Abbot Gyōson
    (1055-1136)

    Lone wild cherry tree,
  We live here in compassion
    Just for each other.
  Who but I knows of your flowers?
  Who but you knows of my tears?

Zakura, having a double meaning, "cherry" or "you" (female), suggests a broken love story behind his running away into the forest. Great-grandson of Emperor Sanjō, this poet was talented in music, too, and wrote a famous diary.

67

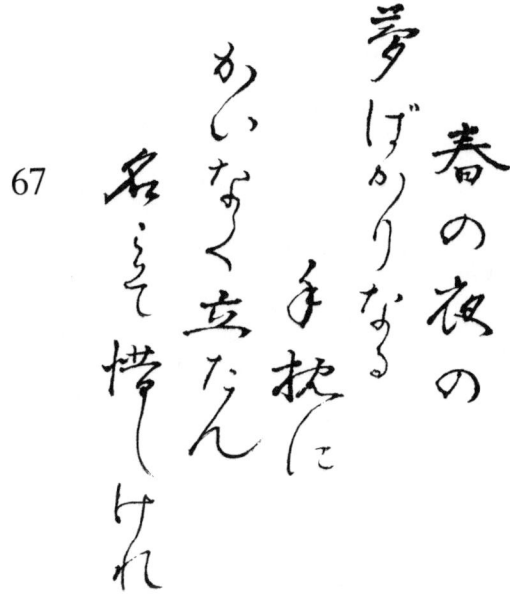

Haru no yo no
Yume bakari naru
 Ta-makura ni
Kainaku tatan
Na koso oshi kere

  Lady Suō (late eleventh century)

This spring evening's dream,
Which began as a mere jest
  Of your arm offered
To pillow my head upon,
Threatens my precious good name.

The story is that, when the ladies were chatting late, she said, "If only I had a pillow!" A man in the next room stuck his arm under the screen into their room and said, "Use this." The buildings were that flimsy.

68

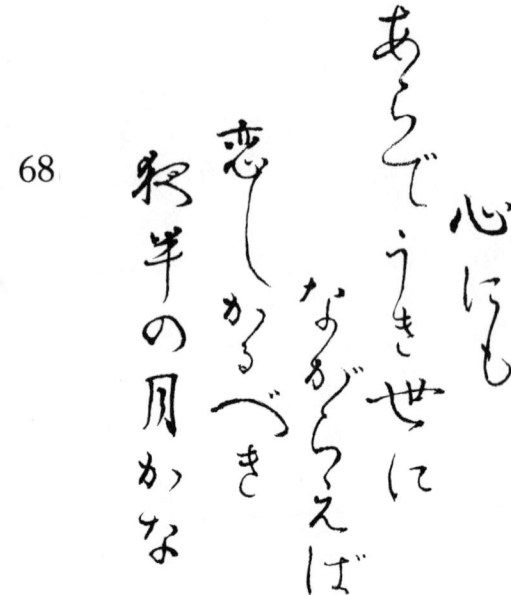

Kokoro ni mo
Arade uki yo ni
   Nagaraeba
Koishikaru beki
Yowa no tsuki kana
     Emperor Sanjō (976-1017)

          Yes, I may yet live
          Years and years in this crass world
              Against my wishes,
          For, if not, how I should miss
          The rise of the midnight moon!

Though that is the literal translation, *Koishikaru beki* has a second meaning: in this world of status grabbers and fighters, who know nothing of civilized values,
   Persons with love in their hearts
   Can still see the midnight moon.
This appears to have been written after he was deposed by a gang of crooks and had suffered other misfortunes.

69

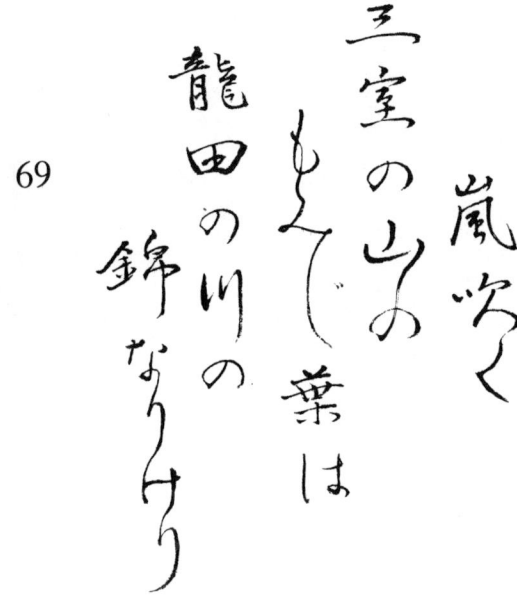

Arashi fuku
Mimuro no yama no
Momiji-ba wa
Tatsuta no kawa no
Nishiki nari keri

The Monk Nōin (988-1052)

See how last night's storm,
Shaking down the maple leaves
 From Three Cave Mountain,
Has garbed in a rich brocade
Our poor Dragon Field River!

From monk or emperor, these last two poems, beautifully paired, underline the this-world focus of their nation's mental life at a time when Europe was heavily bent the other way.

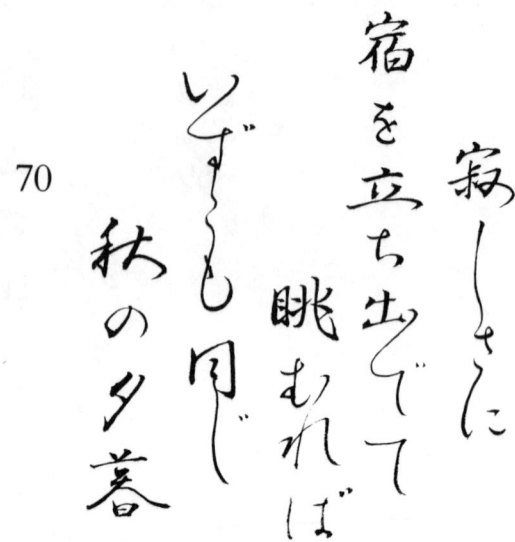

Sabishisa ni
Yado wo tachi idete
  Nagamureba
Izuko mo onaji
Aki no yūgure

  The Monk Ryōzen (early eleventh century)

Feeling my loneness,
I get up, leave the house, go,
  Look at many things.
Everywhere it is the same,
Dusk at the end of autumn.

Late autumn in many cultures has been a symbol of endings and regrets. The text of this poem has appeared in several variants, though the meaning is clear.

71

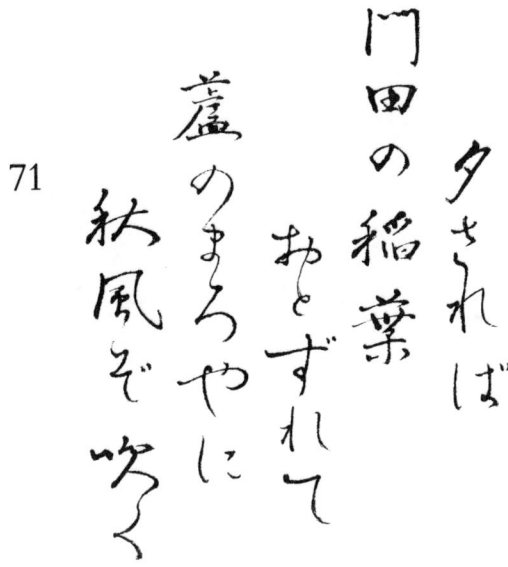

Yū sareba
Kado ta no inaba
Otozurete
Ashi no maroya ni
Aki kaze zo fuku

Chief Minister Tsunenobu
(1016-1097)

Promptly with evening
In the field before my door,
Rattling the rice leaves,
Then banging at this reed hut,
The noise of the autumn wind.

What this lordly fellow was doing in a simple hut is not known, but his experience reminds us of poem 1, written 400 years earlier. What emerges here is that this traveler, a musician noted for his performances on the lutelike *biwa*, is in this collection almost the only poet so aware of sounds.

72

Oto ni kiku
Takashi no hama no
　Adanami wa
Kakeji ya sode no
Nure mo koso sure

Lady-in-Waiting Kii (mid-eleventh century)

Oh, yes, I hear them
Booming on Great Teacher Beach,
　All those noisy waves.
They come almost close enough
To wet my long, trailing sleeves.

The reference is to a saying: Shallow water makes noisy waves. How about a shallow man? The first line means either, "I hear them," or, "Your reputation is known." *Sure* at the end is a pun, "close" or "knowledgeable." She knows a bit too much to wet her sleeves weeping for such a dandy.

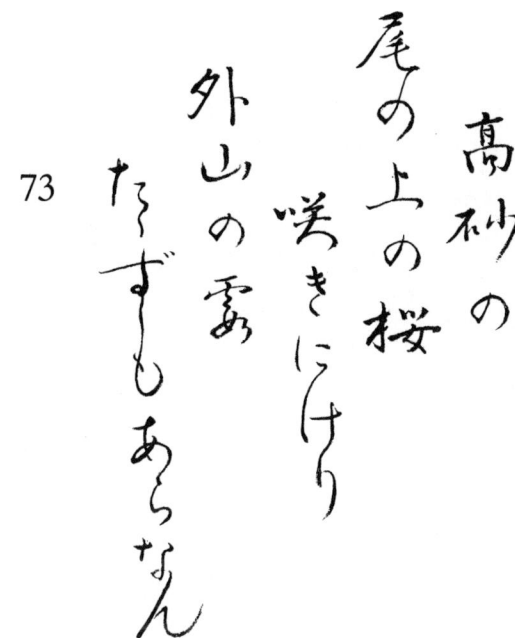

Takasago no
Onoe no sakura
  Saki ni keri
Toyama no kasumi
Tatazu mo aranan

    Ōe no Masafusa (1041-1111)

    The white cherry tree
  On the ridge of Great Sand Hill,
    How fully it blooms!
  Please, O lowering mountain clouds,
  Do not rouse yourselves just now!

This occasional poem is redeemed by its playful tone and by its skillful repetition of sounds. We note *sa* three times, *no* three times followed by *mo*, and subtler effects: *ki* . . . *nike*, and *saku* . . . *kasu*, and so on. It can be sung.

74

Ukari keru
Hito wo hasse no
　Yama oroshi
Hageshi kare to wa
Inoranu mono wo

　　Minamoto no Toshiyori (1055-1129)

This wild mountain wind
From Head of Rapids temple,
　As brisk and chilling
As she not looking my way,
Is this what I prayed for there?

The name *Hasse*, "Head of Rapids," divides into *hatsu se*, and *hatsu* with *ino* further down means "New Year's Day prayers," identifying the place (now Long Valley Temple), where one went on January first to pray for success in love. Historically religion has been a part of life and has served all human purposes.

75

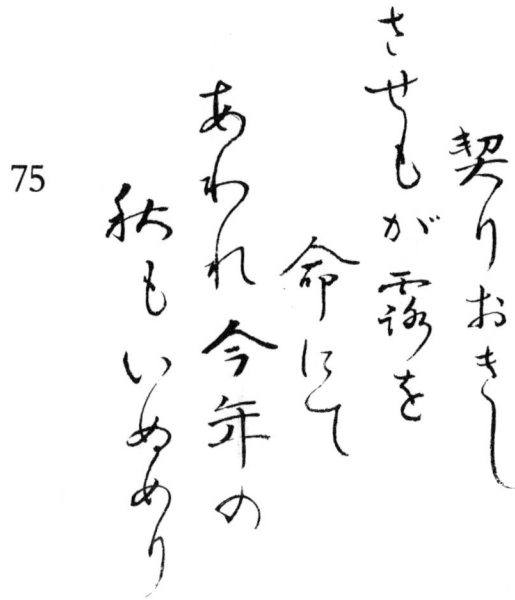

Chigiri okishi
Sasemo ga tsuyu wo
Inochi nite
Aware kotoshi no
Aki mo inumeri

Fujiwara no Mototoshi (1060-1142)

Your vow, my son, came
Like dew on the herbs of life
That brings us repose.
Yet in my declining years
One more autumn has gone by.

Since the father, reminding his son of that promise to work hard in public office, uses the word *chigiri*, commonly a boy's promise to a girl, we divine what is distracting the lad.

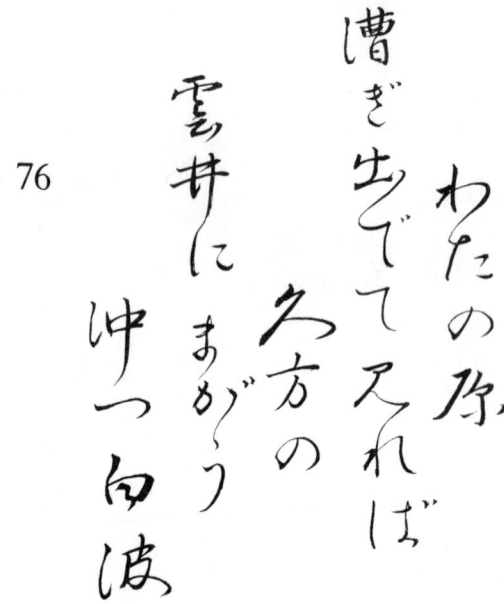

Wata no hara
Kogi idete mireba
　Hisakata no
Kumoi ni magau
Okitsu shira nami

　　Fujiwara no Tadamichi
　　(1097-1164)

　　　　Since I have embarked
　　　On the meadows of the sea
　　　　The sky when I look
　　　Does not tell where the cloud wells
　　　End and the white waves begin.

Punning on *Hisakata*, "eternal sky" or Nara, and *kumoi*, "cloud wells" or the Imperial Court, here is another gentleman from the landlocked capital overwhelmed by the ocean. On a day when the horizon vanished, doubtless in summer, this traveler does not actually say that he was frightened.

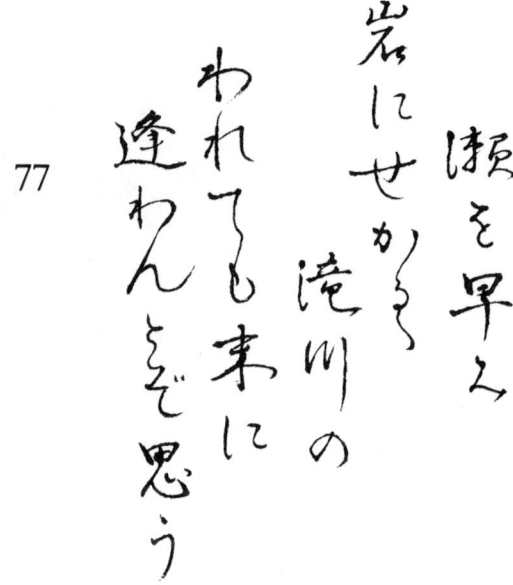

Se wo hayami
Iwa ni sekaruru
  Takigawa no
Warete mo sue ni
Awan to zo omou

  Emperor Sutoku (1119-1164)

Because the river
Swiftly pours over these rocks,
  It divides in two;
Yet in the end these fragments
Will rush to meet each other.

When young, he fell in love, but upon becoming Emperor, found himself embroiled in civil war, with the girl's family on the opposing side.

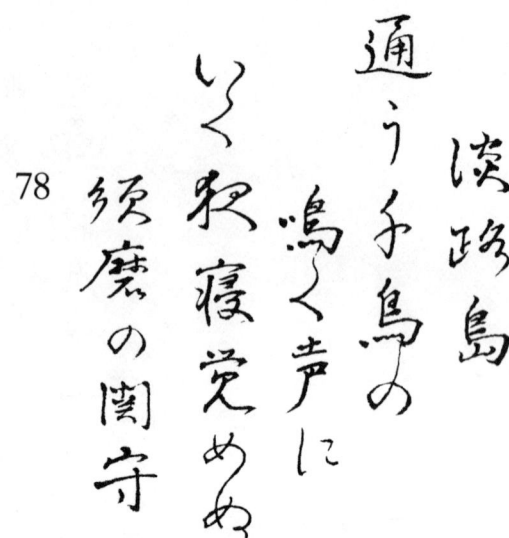

Awaji shima
Kayou chidori no
Naku koe ni
Iku yo nezamenu
Suma no sekimori

    Minamoto no Kanemasa (d. 1112)

Flitting like our lives,
How often do these crying
Thousands of plovers
Make you restless in the night,
O guardsmen at Fate's barrier?

The little birds flew between the island of Awaji (transitory ways) and the Gate of Suma (as inevitable as a grindstone).

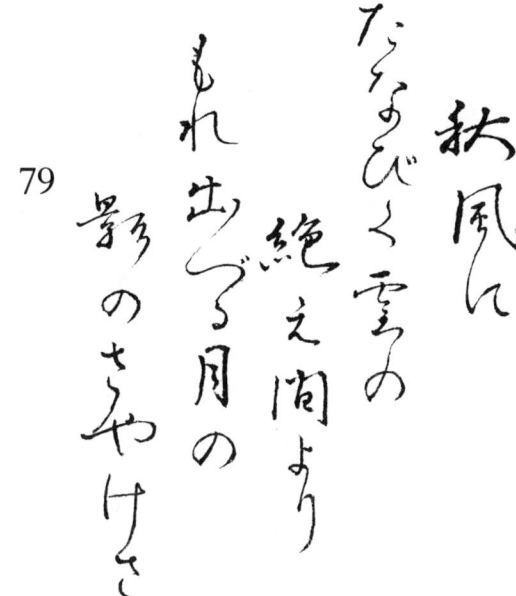

79

Aki kaze ni
Tanabiku kumo no
  Taema yori
More-izuru tsuki no
Kage no sayakesa

  Fujiwara no Akisuke (1090-1154)

  In this autumn wind
  That flings its tent roof of clouds
    Across the evening
  A tattered rent lets escape
  The full, bright disk of the moon.

Tana no longer means a tent, but did then. It seems, perhaps, embarrassing that by the twelfth century these Court officials far across a then unknown sea had achieved a degree of awareness (from Buddhism) that European poets and painters would not attempt until the American and French Revolutions.

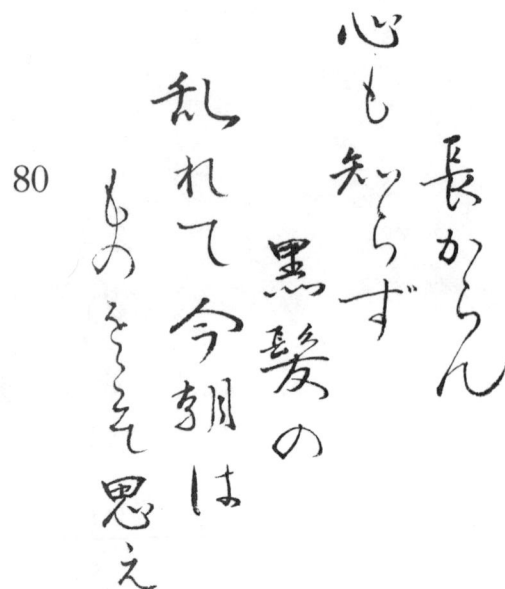

*Naga karan
Kokoro mo shirazu
Kuro kami no
Midarete kesa wa
Mono wo koso omoe*

Lady Horikawa (early twelfth century)

Whether his heart will
To the end remain captive
To my long black hair
I do not know this morning
With my hair in rebellion.

In the classical literature this is one of the very rare hints we get that Japanese lovemaking, in spite of all those clothes and all that formality, was as athletic as ours.

81

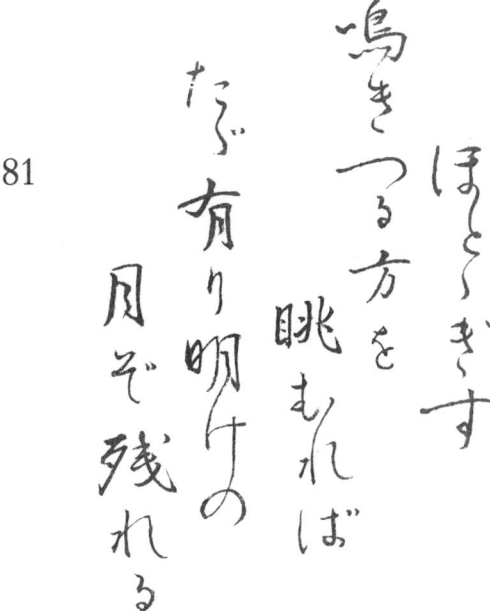

Hototo gisu
Nakitsuru kata wo
Nagamureba
Tada ariake no
Tsuki zo nokoreru

Fujiwara no Sanesada (1139-1191)

When I looked to see
How one tiny cuckoo bird
Could make all that song,
The moon of early morning,
But only the moon, remained.

Musically a remarkable poem. English cannot match such effects as *kitsu* in the second line preparing *tsuki* in the last, nor are our ears trained to hear *ki* and *gi* as the same, *ta* and *da*, and so on.

82

思ひわび
さても命は
あるものを
憂きに堪えぬは
涙なりけり

Omoi wabi
Satemo inochi wa
Aru mono wo
Uki ni taenu wa
Namida nari keri

The Monk Dōin (d. ca. 1180)

Yes, I think too much
About my lone, wretched life
Since I must lose you,
But how does one linger on
When one has nothing but tears?

This court official loved a lady to whom he must not declare himself. When she was to marry someone else, he resigned and withdrew from the world. His father was not the same class as hers.

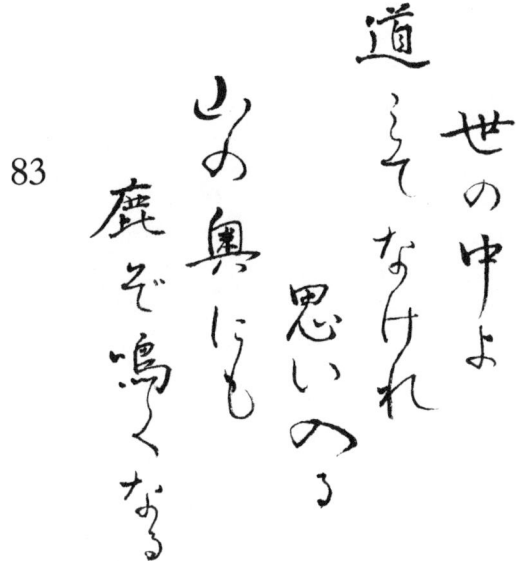

83

Yo no naka yo
Michi koso nakere
  Omoi iru
Yama no oku ni mo
Shika zo naku naru

    Fujiwara no Toshinari
    (1114-1204)

        I begin to see
That in the whole world there are
    Only paths to grief.
Even here deep in the hills
I hear the wild deer crying.

This may be a self-conscious echo of poem 5, the authors having achieved the same rank in the priesthood. Tutor to several Court notables, this poet had been promoted to high position but had left it all, retired into the forest as a monk, and there composed this tanka in such violent terms that it was disapproved as indecent, even unpatriotic. His son was the anthologist, who deliberately chose this as a test piece: if you could not believe Court grandeur was sometimes that inhuman, that was up to you.

84

永らえば
またこのごろや
しのばれん
憂しと見し世ぞ
今は恋しき

Nagaraeba
Mata konogoro ya
Shinobaren
Ushi to mishi yozo
Ima wa koishiki

Fujiwara no Kiyosuke (1104-1177)

After I have lived
A long time I may recall
Nostalgically,
Perhaps even with longing,
All these tough, trying struggles.

How can you live quietly and write poems when your father, Emperor Rokujō, wants you to push ahead in administrative grandeur? And will you not one day miss the glamor? And do you not love the old pest really?

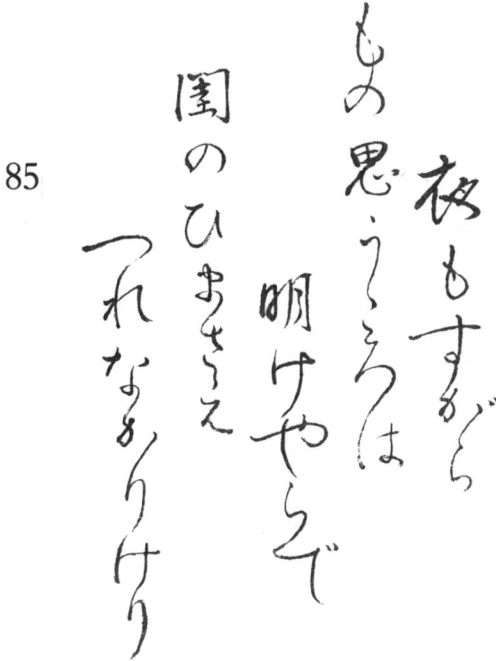

Yo mo sugara
Mono omou koro wa
  Ake yarade
Neya no hima sae
Tsure nakari keri

    The Monk Shun-e (b. 1113)

        Which is more chilling,
      Day withering into night,
         The glimmer of dawn
    Through some chink in a bedroom,
    This time of anxiety?

The pun on *koro*, which can mean "this moment" or "this era," adds a dimension as pertinent as each reader cares to see.

86

Nageke tote
Tsuki ya wa mono wo
　　Omowasuru
Kakochi-gao naru
Waga namida kana

　　The Monk Saigyo (1118-1190)　　The moon to me now
　　　　　　　　　　　　　　　　Is a thing to be deplored,
　　　　　　　　　　　　　　　　　　Forcing me to think
　　　　　　　　　　　　　　　　Till my face grows drawn and tense,
　　　　　　　　　　　　　　　　And I feel the tears begin.

In youth a much-praised army captain, but at twenty-three fed up with pointless slaughter, he turned monk, built himself huts in several places. He became a great hiker, carried a backpack, blazed his path through forests by breaking a twig or branch here and there but often would next time try a different route just for fun. Yet even he, if he remembered too much, could be shaken.

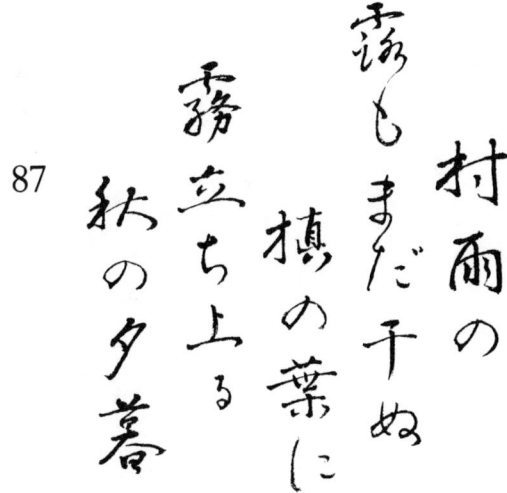

Murasame no
Tsuyu mo mada hinu
　Maki no ha ni
Kiri tachi noboru
Aki no yūgure

　　The Monk Jakuren (1139?-1202?)

　　　　The jewels from that
　　　　Rustic shower still glitter
　　　　　Among the needles
　　　　Of the teak trees as the mist
　　　　Of autumn evening rises.

The Japanese so-called teak tree, also called Chinese pine, has always looked to me like our redwoods, the tall kind, and old. Like the rest of these poet-monks, he is recalling Court life, to which he refers obliquely by his insistence on *murasame*, "village rain," a word commonly used for a passing shower.

88

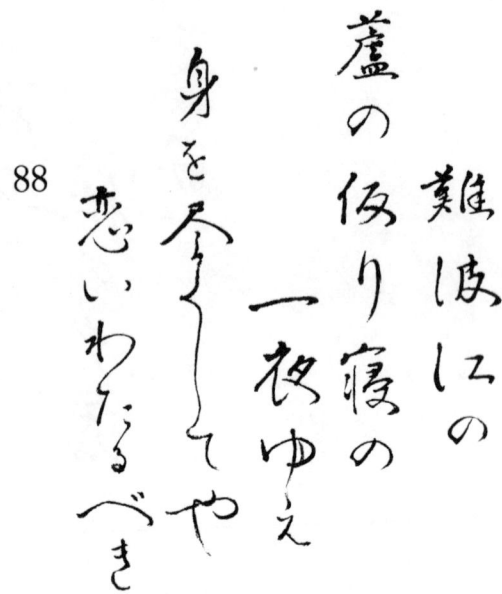

*Naniwa e no
Ashi no karine no
　Hito yo yue
Mi wo tsukushite ya
Koi wataru beki*

Stewardess of the Empress Kōka
(twelfth century)

Because of one night,
A lovers' nap on those reeds
　Of Naniwa Bay,
Ought I, giving my body,
Love you always, do you think?

This astonishing poem has opposite meanings depending on our assumptions. "Because of one night I shall pine for you always," if we think that way. But *beki* means "ought to do," not "will do." And the question mark *ya* is attached to giving herself. At a poets' meeting where the assigned theme was "love while traveling," chosen obviously by a showoff wanting to shock people, this lady answered him right back by improvising a tanka more shocking than his silly question. She said it was fiction.

89

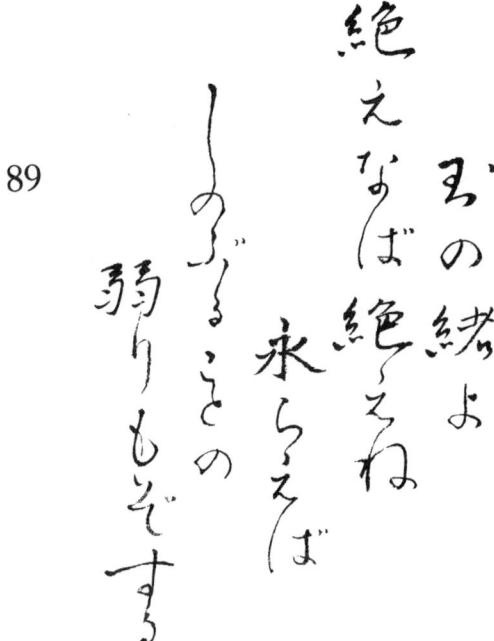

Tama no o yo
Taenaba taene
　Nagaraeba
Shinoburu koto no
Yowari mo zo suru

　　Princess Shokushi (d. 1201)

O my string of gems,
If you can break, break at once!
For should I live long
This heavy hiding of love
Would become frayed and empty.

The powerful metaphor of life as precious as gems is enforced, to Japanese ears, by the repeated *ta*, abruptly shifted to the softness of *shinoburu* and *yowari*, so that the sounds tell as much of the meaning as do the words. A forbidden love was terrible for a princess.

90

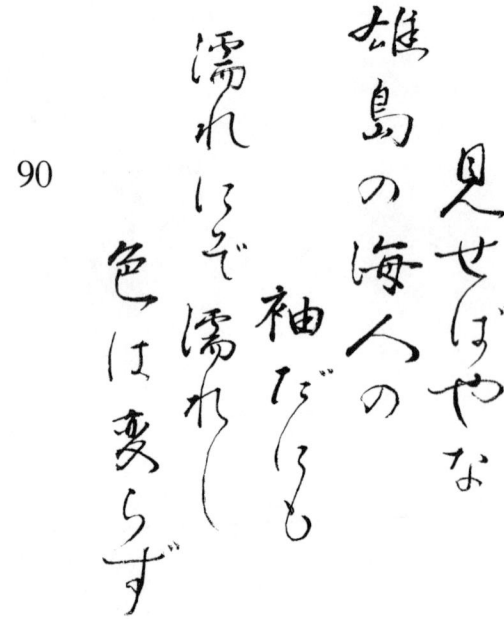

Misebayana
Ojima no ama no
  Sode dani mo
Nure ni zo nureshi
Iro wa kawarazu

    Lady-in-Waiting Sukeko
    (fl. ca. 1200)

Here I sit longing
To show you the fishermen
  Of Valiant Island,
How their sleeves, though wet each day,
Do not change color so much.

This poem, to which translators usually add something, is in fact all a metaphor, carrying to a limit the convention that wet sleeves represent tears and tears are for neglected love. We are to apply the metaphor; the poet explains nothing. The old word *ama*, "fishermen" or "waterbugs," adds the connotation that persons in humble walks of life had not the restrictions that she did.

91

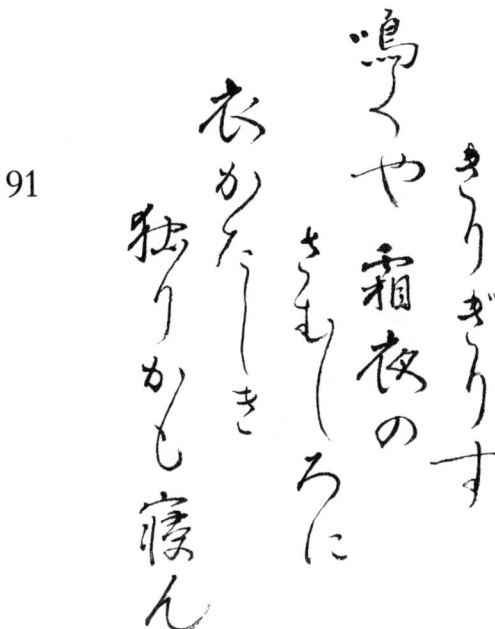

Kirigirisu
Naku ya shimo yo no
  Samushiro ni
Koromo katashiki
Hitori kamo nen

The Regent Fujiwara no Yoshitsune
(1169-1206)

On your sleeping mat
This night when the crickets' cry
  Is predicting frost
Must you spread only one side
Of your robe for you alone?

Surely one of the most amiable amatory verses in this collection. As the poem has no pronouns "my" and "I" can be substituted for "your" and "you." The meaning is the same. We still tell temperature by the crickets, if we have been trained to listen.

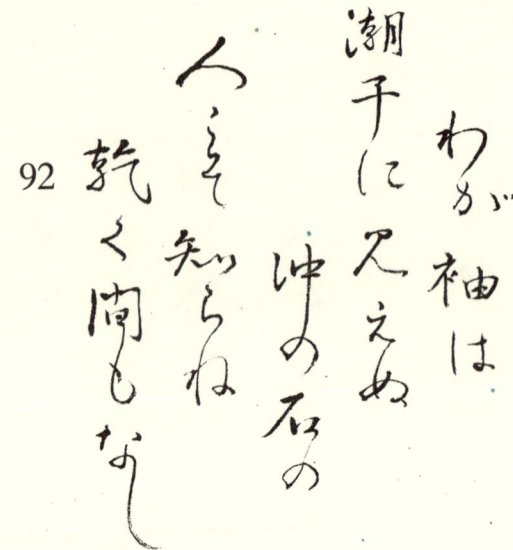

Waga sode wa
Shiohi ni mienu
　Oki no ishi no
Hito koso shirane
Kawaku ma mo nashi

　　Lady Sanuki (fl. ca. 1200)

　　　　Like a rock out there
　　　　In the open sea, unseen
　　　　　　Even at low tide,
　　　　My sleeve, though nobody knows,
　　　　Finds no place to go to dry.

She married Emperor Nijō. He retired; she renounced the world as a Shinto nun. *Oki no ishi,* "a rock in the sea," became after this poem a traditional expression for a grieving heart.

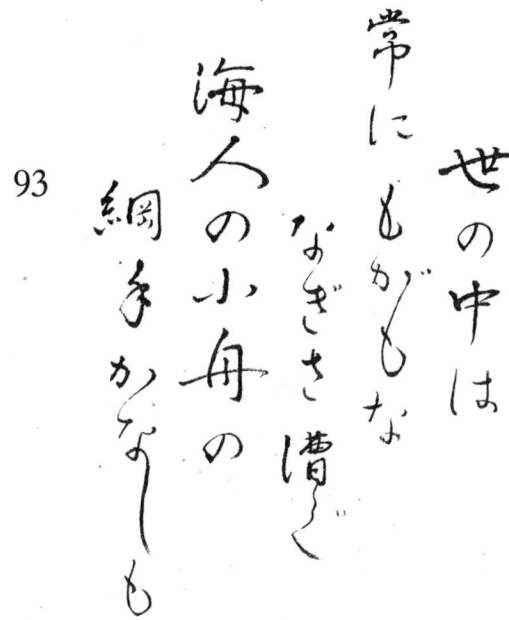

93

Yo no naka wa
Tsune ni mo gamo na
   Nagisa kogu
Ama no obune no
Tsunade kanashi mo

   Minamoto no Sanetomo (1192-1219)

Oh, to be always
Here in this world as it is
   Where mere fishermen
Tugging on their little boat
Can be so touching to me!

Tsune has a double meaning, "forever" or "ordinary." Both Shinto and Buddhism were teaching people, a thousand years before any such doctrine appeared in the West, to appreciate the beauty of the everyday, inexpensive things. For this military leader to do so was easier than for the fishermen themselves.

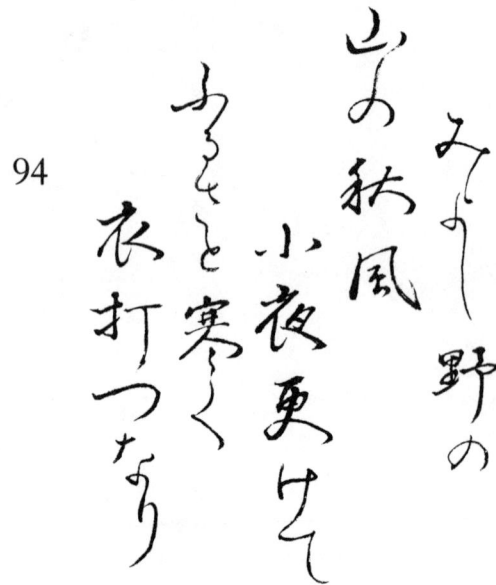

Miyoshino no
Yama no aki kaze
  Sayo fukete
Furu sato samuku
Koromo utsu nari

Fujiwara no Masatsune (1170-1221)

Dusk and autumn wind
From Beautiful-Luck-Field Hill,
  My little village,
The dismal chill, sounds of cloth
Beaten by women's mallets.

This time the use of the place-name reveals that these poets understood irony. In Japan as in Europe, several kinds of cloth were moistened with fuller's earth and beaten to be made thick and soft. The sound was so gloomy that *Don Quixote* gives a whole chapter to it.

95

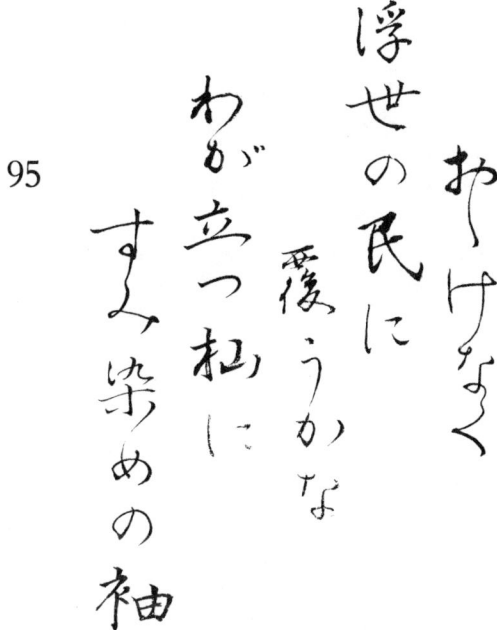

Ōkenaku
Ukiyo no tami ni
Ōukana
Waga tatsu soma ni
Sumizome no sode

Chief Abbot Jien (1155-1225)

The sleeves of my robe,
Black for my Lord Buddha's way,
Are as unsuited
To cover Mt. Hiei
As for most folk in this world.

Aged thirty, he was made head of the temple in the broad forest atop Mt. Hiei. In that tranquillity at a time of war, he felt inadequate and sent this poem to advise a friend not to try it.

96

Hana sasou
Arashi no niwa no
　Yuki narade
Furi yuku mono wa
Waga mi nari keri

　　Fujiwara no Kintsune (1171-1244)

What is falling now
Is not the blossom harvest
　The storm turns to snow
Here in this sheltered garden
But myself, the most secure.

Written in retirement in his famous Golden Pavilion, which seems to float like a dream, mirrored in its pond. *Furi*, the key word, has the same two meanings as in English, "falling" (as snow or rain) or "becoming old." Ex-prime-minister, he was also losing power to the Kamakura shoguns, newcomers then.

97

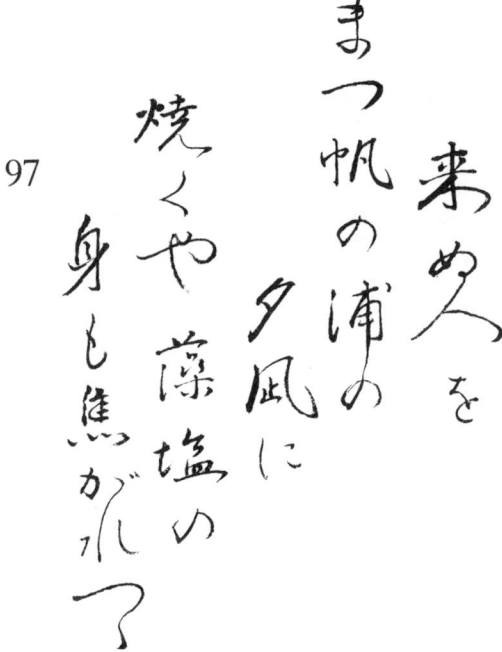

Konu hito wo
Matsu-ho no ura no
   Yū nagi ni
Yaku ya mo shio no
Mi mo kogare tsutsu

Fujiwara no Sadaie (1162-1241)

    Myself as ardent
As the kelp burnt here for salt
    In the evening calm
Of the Cove of Sails, I wait
For her who does not arrive.

The text, stuffed with puns, is so equivocal, the translation should be two-sided. Kelp not being very ardent, he seems to say that, while we are stuck here, let's evoke the beautiful scene, slender smoke columns rising, limp sails on the water. If in the original the poem is a bit limp, we do not complain; the anthologist had to include this one, by himself.

98

Kaze soyogu
Nara no ogawa no
　Yūgure wa
Misogi zo natsu no
Shirushi nari keru

　　Fujiwara no Ietaka (1158-1237)

Rustling the oak leaves
Here over Little River,
　The breeze of twilight
For our lustration gently
Reminds us, summer has come.

This annual ceremony is quiet, relaxed, inviting perceptions. Just as, even on warm days, we do not feel that winter is gone until the oaks put out leaves (the *nara* being a late-leafing variety), so he had not thought of his daughter as grown up till suddenly she was to be married. The poem is for that occasion.

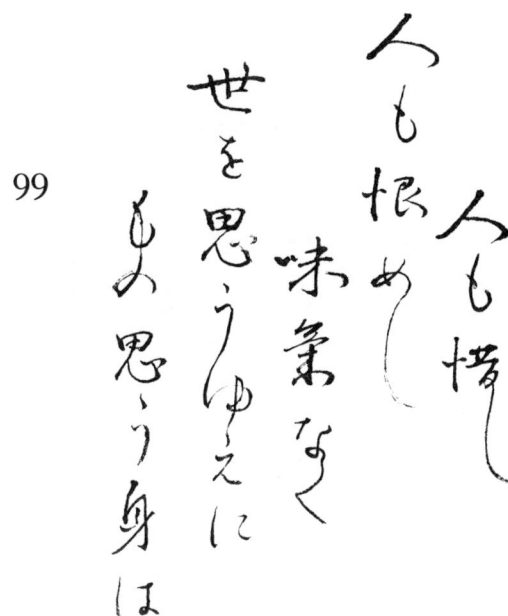

Hito mo oshi
Hito mo urameshi
  Ajiki naku
Yo wo omou yue ni
Mono omou mi wa

Retired Emperor Gotoba (1180-1239)

Sorry not to see
Some people and sorrier
  To see some others,
In my inmost self I feel
The world has lost its savor.

Perhaps an emperor has the right to say outright what many of us try to push out of our minds. "Retired" is a euphemism, Gotoba having been exiled by a rival faction. A boy on the throne, he never had a chance. Even his name is ill-omened, literally "bird feather left behind," which, under other circumstances, could have been beautiful.

100

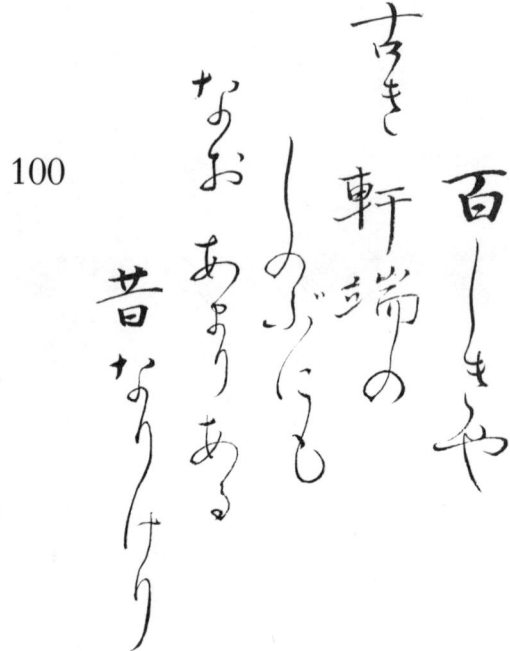

Momo shiki ya
Furuki nokiba no
Shinobu ni mo
Nao amari aru
Mukashi nari keri

Emperor Juntoku (1197-1242)

In these ancient eaves,
Built of so many hundreds
Of stones, the bracken
Growing wild bring back sadly
The glories of long ago.

Reading of earlier years, before the shoguns took away the power of government to Kamakura, he wrote this while he was twenty. *Shinobu* is a fernlike plant or "to remember." Later, remembering his father, Gotoba, Juntoku plotted revenge, was revealed by spies, and was exiled also. The anthologist ends his book with these glum musings on his era, so much like our own.

AN INDEX AND GLOSSARY OF POETS

Abe no Nakamaro, 7
Akazome Emon, 59
Ariwara no Narihira, Ason (Lord, courtier without specific duties), 17
Ariwara no Yukihira, Chūnagon (Middle Councilor), brother of Ariwara no Narihira (17), 16
Dōin Hōshi (monk), 82
Egyō Hōshi (monk), or Eikei Hōshi, 47
Fujiwara no Akisuke, Sakyō no Daibu (Courtier of the Fifth Rank), 79
Fujiwara no Asatada, Chūnagon (Middle Councilor), son of Fujiwara no Sadakata (25), 44
Fujiwara no Atsutada, Gon Chūnagon (Middle Councilor in Power), 43
Fujiwara no Go-Kyōgoku (or Yoshitsune), Sesshō Saki no Daijō Daijin (former Prime Minister and Regent), 91
Fujiwara no Ietaka, Jūni-i (Junior Grade, Second Rank), adopted son of Jakuren Hōshi (87), 98
Fujiwara no Kanesuke, Chūnagon (Middle Councilor), 27

Fujiwara no Katako, Daini Sammi (Courtier of the Third Rank), so-called for her husband; daughter of Murasaki Shikibu (57), 58
Fujiwara no Kintō, Dainagon (Chief Councilor), 55
Fujiwara no Kintsune, Nyūdō Saki no Daijō Daijin (Lay Priest, former Prime Minister), 96
Fujiwara no Kiyosuke, Ason (Lord), son of Fujiwara no Akisuke (79), 84
Fujiwara no Koretada, Kentoku Kō (Prince), 45
Fujiwara no Masatsune, Sangi (Councilor), 94
Fujiwara no Michimasa, Sakyō no Daibu (Courtier of the Fifth Rank), 63
Fujiwara no Michinobu, Ason (Lord), nephew of Fujiwara no Yoshitaka (50), 52
Fujiwara no Mototoshi, 75
Fujiwara no Okikaze, 34
Fujiwara no Sadaie (or Teika), Gon Chūnagon (Middle Councilor in Power), son of Fujiwara no Toshinari (83), 97
Fujiwara no Sadayori, Gon Chūnagon (Middle Councilor in Power), son of Fujiwara no Kintō (55), 64
Fujiwara no Sadakata, Sanjō no Udaijin (Third-rank Councilor on the Right), 25
Fujiwara no Sanekata, Ason (Lord), 51
Fujiwara no Sanesada, Gotoku Daiji no Sadaijin (Assistant High Councilor on the Left), 81
Fujiwara no Tadahira, Teishin Kō (Prince), 26
Fujiwara no Tadamichi, Hōshōji Nyūdō Saki no Kanpaku Daijō Daijin (former Prime Minister), 76
Fujiwara no Toshinari (or Shunzei), Kōdai Gōgū no Daibu (Gentleman-in-Waiting to Prince Gōgū), 83
Fujiwara no Toshiyuki, Ason (Lord), 18
Fujiwara no Yoshitaka, son of Fujiwara no Koretada (45), 50
Funya no Asayasu, 37
Funya (or Bunya) no Yasuhide, 22
Gidō Sanshi no Haha (Mother of Triple Councilor Gidō), Takako, or Kō Naishi (Lady-in-Waiting), 54
Gotoba In (retired Emperor Gotoba), 99
Harumichi no Tsuraki, 32
Inbu Mon-in no Taifu Sukeko (Sukeko, Lady-in-Waiting to Empress Inbu), daughter of Fujiwara no Bunari, 90
Ise, Chō-uke (Favorite), 19
Ise no Taifu (Lady-in-Waiting), or Taisuke, or Ōsuke, 61

Izumi Shikibu (Ceremonies, an abbreviation for several Court titles), sister-in-law of Sanjō In (68), 56
Jakuren Hōshi, 87
Jitō Tennō (Empress), daughter of Tenji Tennō (1), 2
Juntoku In, son of Gotoba (99), 100
Kakinomoto no Hitomaro, 3
Ki no Tomonori, 33
Ki no Tsurayuki, 35
Kisen Hōshi (monk), 8
Kiyohara no Fukayabu, 36
Kiyohara no Motosuke, father of Sei Shōnagon (62), 42
Kōka Mon-in no Betō (Stewardess of Empress Kōka), 88
Kōkō Tennō (Emperor), 15
Koshikibu no Naishi (Lady-in-Waiting), 60
Mibu no Tadami, son of Mibu no Tadamine (30), 41
Mibu no Tadamine, 30
Minamoto no Hitoshi, Sangi (Councilor), 39
Minamoto no Kanemasa, 78
Minamoto no Muneyuki, Ason (Lord), 28
Minamoto no Sanetomo, Shōgun, known as Kamakura no Daijin (commander at Kamakura), 93
Minamoto no Shigeyuki, 48
Minamoto no Tōru, Kawara (Riverbed) no Sadaijin (Chief Councilor on the Left), 14
Minamoto no Toshiyori, Ason (Lord), son of Minamoto no Tsunenobu (71), 74
Minamoto no Tsunenobu, Dainagon (Chief Minister), 71
Motoyoshi Shinnō (Prince), son of Yōzei In (13), 20
Murasaki Shikibu (Purple Ceremonies—see Izumi Shikibu), 57
Nijō-in no Sanuki, wife of retired Emperor-Nijō, 92
Nōin Hōshi (monk), 69
Ōe no Chisato, 23
Ōe no Masafusa, Saki no Chūnagon (former Middle Councilor), 73
Ōnakatomi no Yoshinobu, Ason (Lord), 49
Ono no Komachi, adopted daughter of Ono no Takamura (11), Ono (Little Field), Komachi (Small Town), 9
Ono no Takamura, Sangi (Councilor), 11
Ōshiko-uchi no Mitsune, 29
Ōtomo no Yakamochi, Chūnagon (Middle Councilor), 6

Ryōzen Hōshi (monk), 70
Sagami, 65
Saigyo Hōshi, 86
Saka-no-ue no Korenori, 31
Saki no Daisōjō Jien (former Chief Abbot Jien), son of Fujiwara no Tadamichi (76), 95
Saki no Daisōjō Gyōson (former Chief Abbot Gyōson), 66
Sanjō In (retired Emperor), 68
Sarumaru Dayū (Courtier of the Fifth Rank; later a monk), 5
Sei Shōnagon, daughter of Kiyohara no Motosuke (42), 62
Semimaru, 10
Shokushi (or Shikishi) Naishinnō (Princess Shokushi), daughter of Emperor Gōshirakawa, 89
Shun-e Hōshi (monk), 85
Sone no Yoshitada, 46
Sugawara no Michizane, Kanke (Reed House), 24
Suō no Naishi (Lady-in-Waiting), 67
Sutoku In (retired Emperor), 77
Taiken Mon-in no Horikawa (Horikawa, Lady-in-Waiting to the Empress-Mother Taiken), 80
Taira no Kanemori, 40
Tenji Tennō (Emperor), 1
Udaishō Michitsuna no Haha (Mother of Commander Michitsuna), 53
Ukon (lit. "Near on the Right"), daughter of Shoshō Suenawa, Councilor on the Right, 38
Yamabe no Akahito, 4
Yoshimine no Harutoshi, Sosei Hōshi (monk), son of Yoshimine no Munesada (12), 21
Yoshimine no Munesada, Sōjō Henjō (Abbot Henjō), 12
Yōzei In (retired Emperor), 13
Yūshi Naishinnō-ke Kii (Lady Kii, Lady-in-Waiting to Princess Yūshi), 72

THE LOCKERT LIBRARY OF POETRY IN TRANSLATION

George Seferis: Collected Poems (1924-1955), translated, edited, and introduced by Edmund Keeley and Philip Sherrard

Collected Poems of Lucio Piccolo, translated and edited by Brian Swann and Ruth Feldman

C. P. Cavafy: Collected Poems, translated by Edmund Keeley and Philip Sherrard and edited by George Savidis

Benny Andersen: Selected Poems, translated by Alexander Taylor

Selected Poetry of Andrea Zanzotto, translated and edited by Ruth Feldman and Brian Swann

Poems of René Char, translated by Mary Ann Caws and Jonathan Griffin

Selected Poems of Tudor Arghezi, translated and edited by Michael Impey and Brian Swann

"The Survivor" and Other Poems by Tadeusz Różewicz, translated and introduced by Magnus J. Krynski and Robert A. Maguire

"Harsh World" and Other Poems by Ángel González, translated by Donald D. Walsh.

Dante's "Rime," translated and introduced by Patrick S. Diehl

Ritsos in Parentheses, translations and introduction by Edmund Keeley

Salamander: Selected Poems of Robert Marteau, translated and introduced by Anne Winters

Angelos Sikelianos. Selected Poems, translated and introduced by Edmund Keeley and Philip Sherrard

The Dawn Is Always New: Selected Poetry of Rocco Scotellaro, translated by Ruth Feldman and Brian Swann

Selected Later Poems of Marie Luise Kaschnitz, translated by Lisel Mueller

Osip Mandelstam's "Stone," translated and introduced by Robert Tracy

The Man I Pretend To Be: "The Colloquies" and Selected Poems of Guido Gozzano, translated and edited by Michael Palma, with an introductory essay by Eugenio Montale

Sounds, Feelings, Thoughts: Seventy Poems by Wisława Szymborska, translated and introduced by Magnus J. Krynski and Robert A. Maguire

Gunnar Ekelöf: Songs of Something Else, translated by James Larson and Leonard Nathan

Library of Congress Cataloging in Publication Data
Ogura hyakunin isshu. English.
The little treasury of one hundred people, one poem each.
(Lockert library of poetry in translation)
Translation of: Ogura hyakunin isshu.
Includes index.
    1. Waka—Translations into English. 2. Japanese poetry—To 1600—Translations into English. 3. English poetry—Translations from Japanese. I. Fujiwara, Sadaie, 1162-1241. II. Galt, Thomas Franklin, 1908- . III. Title. IV. Series.
PL758.5.O4E5 1982   895.6'11'08   81-48140
ISBN 0-691-06514-4   AACR2
ISBN 0-691-01392-6 (pbk.)

PL758.5   G81363 $13.50
.04E5   The little treasury of one hundred people,
1982   one poem each.

Please Do Not Remove Card From Pocket

YOUR LIBRARY CARD
may be used at all library agencies. You are, of course, responsible for all materials checked out on it. As a courtesy to others please return materials promptly — before overdue penalties are imposed.

The SAINT PAUL PUBLIC LIBRARY